Ketogenic Diet

The Complete How-To Guide

For Beginners

Robert Wilson

Table of contents

This page has been intentionally left blank

Introduction

Are you feeling fat, sick, and tired? Or maybe just sick and tired of feeling fat?

If so, I know exactly how you feel! I spent most of my life hating what I saw in the mirror and feeling ashamed of the number I saw on the scale. More than that, however, my health was in shambles and I felt tired all the time.

My name is Robert Wilson and I'm here to share with you how I went from living a life of shame and disappointment to transforming my health and changing how I live for the better. What's my secret? The ketogenic diet (otherwise known as the keto diet)

The ketogenic diet is not just another fad diet or health trend – you don't have to go on a hunger strike and you don't have to obsess about putting in hours on the treadmill. This diet is actually based on the process of ketosis which essentially turns your body into a fat-burning machine. By making changes to the food you eat, you can switch your body from burning carbs to burning fat for fuel – and not just the fat you eat. You'll be burning off stored body fat as well!

Many people are skeptical when they first hear about the ketogenic diet. After all, how can you possibly lose weight when eating high-fat foods like cheese, red meat, and heavy cream? I understand your skepticism (because I felt that way too!) but I can assure you that it works and that the ketogenic diet might just be the path that you've been looking for.

Okay, so now that you know a little bit about what the ketogenic diet is, you may be wondering just how it can benefit you. Let me start by telling you just how much this diet changed my own life.

Before keto, I was eighty pounds overweight and teetering on the brink of morbid obesity. My blood sugar levels were a rollercoaster of ups and downs and my energy levels were hovering right around zero. I ate three square meals a day but constantly felt hungry and suffered horrible sugar cravings between meals. I had a hard time focusing at work and I was constantly breaking out in the kind of acne you normally see on a 14-year-old boy.

So, how exactly did going keto make effective and impactful changes to how I live? In every thinkable way!

Going on the keto diet was a bit of a struggle for me at first because I had never before counted or bothered with calories, and I had certainly never paid much attention to food labels or nutritional content. If I wanted to eat it, I ate it – it was as simple as that. When I realized that I was headed down a dangerous road toward death and disease, however, I picked myself up and started making changes.

After a few weeks of making keto-friendly swaps for my favorite foods, I started to notice a difference. My pants were just the slightest bit looser – enough that I didn't feel like I was busting out of them. I was skeptical that I had actually lost much weight, but I wanted to keep going.

After another couple of months, I had gotten myself into a good routine for meals and snacks and I was hitting my macronutrient ratios on an almost daily basis. That's when the pounds really started melting away... but that's not all. I also had more energy than I'd had in years and I was able to power through my work days without an afternoon slump. I felt better than I had in a decade!

Now, years later, I feel like a completely new man.

The ketogenic diet helped me go from a massive 310 pounds to a healthy 230. I'm still a big guy but, at 6-foot-2, I feel pretty good about those numbers. Plus, I have significantly reduced my body fat percentage and have built plenty of new muscle. I'm no longer ashamed to look in the mirror, because I see a healthier, fitter me!

At this point you may still be a little doubtful, but I hope that you are also intrigued. Choosing the ketogenic diet was the best decision I've ever made and I am confident that it can help you as much as it helped me.

Now, what do you have to look forward to in this book?

First and foremost, I will state for the record that I am not a medical practitioner in the conventional sense – meaning I am not a licensed doctor. I am however, a regular person who was dealing with medical issues brought on largely by my own neglect in diet and exercise. It was in my own interest to do the research about nutrition, health, and of course the ketogenic diet. I took courses online and offline about the subject and eventually started cooking as well, figuring that I could use the knowledge I had on the diet to create cooking ideas that my palate would like!

In this book you'll receive an in-depth overview of what the ketogenic diet is and how it differs from other diets. This gives you anchoring fundamentals and the motivation to keep going on the diet, especially in the beginning stages when you may not be seeing the results. You'll learn what it means to put your body in a state of ketosis and how to actually achieve it.

The how-to process is broken down in a simple step by step format – I've actually put myself in the shoes of a keto diet beginner while writing it. What would I have wanted to know in order to make the easiest transition into ketosis? You'll find out which foods you can and cannot eat, and how to track your macronutrient portions, or macros. Plus, you'll get a meal plan and a collection of delicious recipes to make your keto journey as smooth as possible.

Okay, so are you ready to get started?

The ketogenic diet has the potential to completely turn your life around, but it only works if you actually work it! So, don't delay a moment longer – turn the page and keep reading to learn how to make the ketogenic diet work for you!

On a side note, this book is not meant to be a pep talk to make you feel good about yourself, while offering little else. I believe that the most important source of motivation you will have would be from you and your body. The signals that your body gives when it luxuriates in the warm bask of ketone-fueled energy will be the positive spur for you to continue on this keto journey, as it has been, and still is, for me.

Chapter 1
Come Closer! It won't bite:
The Ketogenic Diet

The average American follows a diet that is very high in carbohydrates and you could say it is quite unhealthy. Furthermore, two in three Americans are overweight or obese [1]. The connection between these two things is undeniable. But how exactly does the typical Western diet contribute to obesity? There are many ways.

One example provided by the U.S. Department of Agriculture (USDA) is a report that states the average American consumed 20% more calories per day in the year 2000 than they did in the year 1983 [2]. This report puts most of the blame on the increased consumption of red meat, but fast food and processed foods (especially refined carbohydrates) play a role as well.

Generally speaking, the human body is very flexible – it adapts to the kind of diet you follow, finding a way to derive energy and nutrition from whatever foods you offer it. When you follow a diet high in carbohydrates, your body becomes optimized for burning carbs for fuel. Carbohydrates are comprised of sugar molecules linked together and as your body digests the food you eat, those molecules are broken up into glucose molecules which enter the blood stream and are sent throughout the body to the parts that require energy.

One thing you need to know is that there are different types of carbohydrates and your body metabolizes them differently. Simple carbohydrates are things like white bread, sugary candy, and pasta

Robert Wilson

– these foods are broken down easily and the glucose hits your blood stream quickly, causing a spike in blood sugar. Complex carbohydrates like whole grains, on the other hand, take longer to break down which means that they provide a steady stream of energy instead of a quick burst followed by a crash.

The human body is able to burn through carbohydrates fairly quickly but if you consume more carbohydrates than your body can use, what happens to the excess? Your body is unable to store carbohydrates efficiently – this is why they are the first thing to be burned as energy. Any unused carbs are converted into glycogen which is then stored in the muscles and liver. If your body burns through the available carbs and still requires more energy, it will start to burn through your glycogen stores.

But how do extra carbs turn into fat?

When your blood sugar starts to drop, your body sends a signal to release stored glycogen so it can be burned for energy. If you eat so many calories that your body cannot store the excess as glycogen, the liver starts to convert the extra glucose into triglycerides (fats) which can be stored in the fat cells. The more calories you consume without adequate exercise, the more fat your body will store [3].

The ketogenic diet is different from the typical Western diet because it focuses more on fats than on carbohydrates. In fact, it is a low-carb diet that is meant to put your body into a ketogenic state where it recognizes fat as fuel. Keep reading to learn what ketosis is and how it affects the body.

What is Ketosis? How Does It Work?

If you want to understand the process of ketosis, you should think of your body as a machine. Your body is made up of many different parts but they all require fuel in order to work properly. There are different kinds of fuel you can give your body, although some of them work better than others. Carbohydrates, for example, are quick-burning but they aren't the most efficient option. Plus, your body can't store the excess for quick usage. A better, more efficient source of fuel for the body is fat.

When the body switches from burning carbs to burning fats for fuel, it enters a metabolic state which is known as ketosis. In the absence of quick-burning glucose, the energy usage then turns to stored fats in the liver, as well as the fat in other parts of the body. In burning these stored fats, your body produces ketones. Ketones are a type of fatty acid and they can be utilized as energy in much the same way as glucose can.

The ketogenic diet is based on the principle of ketosis and it is structured with the goal of putting the body into a state where it uses ketones as its primary energy source. Basically, you can accomplish this goal by significantly reducing your carbohydrate intake and increasing your fat intake. You should keep protein intake in moderation to ensure that your body burns stored fat for fuel instead of eating into your muscle.

One thing you need to keep in mind with the ketogenic diet is that while fat will become your primary source of fuel, you do need to eat some carbohydrates. Certain organs in the body require glucose (particularly your brain), so you should keep your carb intake minimal, but definitely above zero. That shouldn't be too difficult in this carb plenty world that we live in!

Is This Just Another Fad Diet?

Now that you have a better understanding of ketosis and what the ketogenic diet is, you may be wondering if it is too good to be true. A diet where you get to eat high-fat foods and still lose weight sounds amazing, right? So, it must be just another fad diet that may help you lose weight at first, but you'll gain it all back later and then some.

In truth, that is not at all the case!

The ketogenic diet is unlike fad diets in that it doesn't rely on extreme restriction or strange dietary habits in order to succeed. Okay, so the idea of eating high levels of fat versus carbohydrates may sound a little strange to you, but it is a principle grounded in science and supported by research. Most fad diets are loosely based on some kind of scientific principle, but they are usually so distorted that, if you delve just below the surface, you'll find that they are not all they're cracked up to be.

If you take a look at the science, you'll find that there is a great deal of research to support the benefits of the ketogenic diet. Here are a few examples:

- A 2014 review published in the *International Journal of Environmental Research and Public Health* confirmed the benefits of the ketogenic diet for effective weight loss and improvement in cardiovascular risk factors [4].
- A 2013 study published in the *European Journal of Clinical Nutrition* revealed that the ketogenic diet helps to suppress appetite and supports other benefits for weight loss [5].
- A 2004 study published in *Prostaglandins, Leukotrienes and Essential Fatty Acids* revealed therapeutic effects of the ketogenic diet for insulin resistance, free-radical damage, and hypoxia [6].

- A 2005 study published in the *Annals of Internal Medicine* revealed that a low-carbohydrate diet like the ketogenic diet produced significant improvements in blood glucose levels and insulin resistance [7].
- A 2009 review published in *Obesity Reviews* summarized the benefits of a low-carbohydrate diet for both obesity and cardiovascular disease – it shows significant changes in body mass as well as cholesterol levels, triglycerides, and blood pressure [8].
- A 2007 study published in the *Journal of Nutrition and Metabolism* revealed the benefits of a calorie-restricted ketogenic diet for reducing growth in cases of malignant brain cancer [9].
- A 2010 study published in the Polish journal *Przeglad Lekarski* showed the benefits of a ketogenic diet in reducing epilepsy and protecting the brain [10].

By now it should be clear to you that the ketogenic diet and its benefits are grounded in science and research. But how does it differ from other diets? Keep reading to find out.

How is the Ketogenic Diet Different from Other Diets?

Unlike many fad diets, the ketogenic diet is designed for long-term use. The longer you follow the diet, the more benefits you will receive. Though this diet does offer benefits such as weight loss, improved energy levels, repaired insulin sensitivity, and better mood, it is different from other diets in a number of ways. Here are some quick differences between the ketogenic diet and other popular diets:

- **Atkins Diet** – Though both diets are low in carbohydrates, the keto diet focuses on fat consumption and there are recommended ratios for carbohydrates, protein, and fats. The Atkins diet is more concerned with its four phases, with one leading to short term ketosis. The maintenance phase of the Atkins diet is decidedly not as low carb as you would be on the keto diet.
- **Paleo Diet** – The Paleo diet is grain-free, gluten-free, and dairy-free with an emphasis on fresh fruits, vegetables, nuts, and lean protein. The ketogenic diet focuses more on fatty proteins like red meat as well as dairy products like heavy cream. Both diets are designed for long-term use and provide many health benefits.
- **Mediterranean Diet** – The Mediterranean diet places heavy emphasis on healthy fats (particularly omega-3 fatty acids) but also includes a lot of whole grains and high-carb veggies. Both are intended for long-term use and can support weight loss as well as numerous health benefits.
- **Gluten-Free Diet** – A medical necessity for people with gluten allergies and celiac disease, the gluten-free diet is also a popular health trend. This type of diet is free from gluten-containing grains but there are no other restrictions. There is some overlap between the gluten-free and ketogenic diets because many gluten-free alternatives like almond flour and coconut flour fit well into the low-carb, high-fat keto diet.
- **Clean Eating** – Not a specific diet but a dietary choice, clean eating involves eating only whole, minimally processed foods. This type of diet tends to be high in whole grains, fruits, and veggies which is a departure from the fat-centric ketogenic diet, though both include plenty of protein from healthy sources.

- **Detoxes and Cleanses** – Whether it's juicing, smoothies, or fasting, detox diets and cleanses are usually very low in calories and fat. These diets are designed to cleanse the body of accumulated toxins and to encourage rapid weight loss but most of it ends up being water weight. The ketogenic diet is a long-term choice and doesn't put as much stress on the system as crash diets. Detoxes and cleanses have their place, but should be viewed as tools to optimize body health and not as a long term diet.
- **Vegan and Vegetarian** – These diets limit or exclude animal products such as meat and eggs – the focus is on excluding these foods rather than restricting calories. The ketogenic diet is different because there is a heavy emphasis on animal products like bacon, eggs, and red meat as well as dairy products (which are excluded from the vegan diet).

By now you should have a better understanding of what the ketogenic diet is and how it is different from other diets. In the next chapter, we'll take a closer look at the benefits of the ketogenic diet, some information for fasting while on the diet and some precautions to take before starting off on keto.

Chapter 2
Good for me. Great for You: The Benefits

The most obvious benefit of the ketogenic diet is, of course, weight loss. While you will find that pretty much any diet can help you lose weight if you cut enough calories, the ketogenic diet is optimized specifically for fat loss. If you've been struggling to shed a spare tire or you've been wanting to whittle your waist, the ketogenic diet may be just what you've been looking for.

But how exactly does the ketogenic diet work for weight loss?

The concept is fairly simple. When you reduce your carbohydrate intake so that your body no longer has stored glucose to burn for fuel, it has to find something else to burn. In addition to burning the fat you eat, your body will also start to hack away at your stored fat. Numerous research studies have shown that the ketogenic diet is much more effective in burning fat than low-fat and high-carb diets. The body needs the fats as raw materials to produce ketones for fuel!

In addition to increasing fat burn, the ketogenic diet will also reduce insulin production, so you stop storing fat. That means that even if you do overeat once in a while, you're not going to undo all of the progress you've made with the diet. You will also find that the ketogenic diet reduces your appetite, so you feel less hungry between meals and that will help keep you from snacking and overeating.

All of the above is fine and dandy and of course great to hear, but what exactly is the science behind all these great benefits and more? Let's find out!

Natural Weight Loss

This is pretty much the one of the main drivers for many, many folks taking up the ketogenic diet, at least I know I was also one of them hopping on the bandwagon when I knew I needed weight loss in order to improve my health situation. The ketogenic diet is really great for weight loss, as you will soon find out when you embark on the meal plans and really get into ketosis. The true magic of this is that you engage your body to help you out in losing the weight, instead of relying on calorie counting and restrictions to generate fat burn.

When we first start out on the diet, we will begin to lose water weight in the initial stages. The reason for this is primarily due to our stored carbohydrates being present in mainly liquid glycogen form. As we reduce the reliance on carbohydrates, the body draws down upon these easily available stores of energy first as it grapples with the transition into ketosis. This water weight loss can account for anything from 5 to 20 pounds, depending on your initial starting weight when you begin the keto diet. This is a great morale booster to be sure, and most folks credit the keto diet with the lost weight. If we were to be very exacting in our specifications though, this water weight loss is actually due to us restricting our carbs rather than the actual process of fat burning ketosis.

As we get beyond the first few days and transit into the first few weeks of being on the keto diet, that is when further drops on the weighing scale will definitely be recorded. The key here is the carbohydrate restriction that we have been constantly harping on. As a source of quick fuel, carbs can be second to none. The glucose obtained from the carbs channel quickly into all areas of the body and provide them with the necessary energy boost when needed. The downside for this is that our bodies aren't really built for storing carbs. We really cannot store beyond a day or two of energy unlike our fat stores.

When we cut down on carbs, the body goes into ketosis as we all know by now. This nature's alternate plan for energy would see fats being processed through the liver and then converted into energy giving ketones. That is also part of the reason why some folks actually term the ketogenic diet as a starvation diet. In a sense, they are not wrong, because this alternate way for the body to produce energy actually can sustain a human for up to a month without ingestion of food. The fat stores become the fuel for energy. However, I would definitely have to state most strongly that we are not starving ourselves whilst on the keto diet. Just because ketosis is nature's way of not letting us starve when we are deprived of food does not mean there should be any negative connotations attached to it. More importantly, whilst on the keto diet, we have to remember that we are not really counting calories and it is a definite must to eat when we feel hungry.

When our body successfully transits into burning fat for fuel, this would mean the stored fat as well as the fat that we consume daily would become fair game for ketone production. The trick here is the need to let the body get accustomed to burning fat instead of glucose, which is the main reason why the keto diet is a high fat low carb diet. As long we do not break ourselves out of ketosis, the weight loss that we experience would definitely be from the fats, aside from the initial water weight loss mentioned earlier.

No exercise, no calorie restriction, no weight pills and exotic berries which you need for losing weight. The ketogenic diet simply enlists the body's natural functions in order to kick start this powerful process of natural fat loss. One thing to note however, this does not mean that you get to eat and binge all the way. No matter what methods you use to lose weight, if you were to over eat and consume food even when you feel satiated, I would dare say it would be a tall order to instigate any weight loss if that were the case. Happily, there is something about the ketogenic diet that also helps to prevent over eating. Read on!

Hunger Management

First off, when we wean ourselves from the carb based diet and move on to a fat based one, we are already doing ourselves a favor when it comes to hunger management. Carbs generally call to their own, like the sirens of yore that sailors in ancient times feared so much. Tell me if you have experienced this. You finish a bag of chips or perhaps three chocolate doughnuts, and within an hour or two, your stomach growls a little and there is that little, warmish feeling at the pit of your belly signaling that it is about time to find food again.

The primary cause of this would be due to the blood sugar fluctuations happening whenever there is an over the top intake of glucose. We would be talking more about this in the later segment but it would suffice now to say that when we transit to a primarily fat based diet, this issue with the carbs meddling with the feelings of hunger would go away.

As we move into ketosis and the body activates the fat burning process for energy, we would generally feel less instances of hunger and more feelings of satiety. This occurs even if we were to be eating just two meals in a day, which I must say, is quite common amongst keto practitioners.

As we take in more fat and moderate amounts of protein, these two essential macronutrients have the ability to let you feel satiated and get that feeling of full-ness for longer periods of time than if you were on a carb based diet. Couple this with the fact that the majority of processed and unhealthy foods have plenty of carbs in them, it shouldn't come as too much of a surprise that you would start feeling less hunger as you cut out these empty calories and replace them with nutrient dense whole foods consisting of fat and protein.

Beyond this, being in ketosis actually causes a double whammy effect on the hormones that control hunger pangs. Ghrelin, the hormone that makes us feel hungry, sees its production being muted when our body is in ketosis. This is good news because ghrelin usually increases whenever we engage in any traditional dieting and start losing weight. This would mean that you would be stuck in between a rock and a hard place. The more you try to lose weight via conventional dieting, the more hunger you would feel due to increased ghrelin production! Besides this, the hormone that controls the feeling of satiety, cholecystokinin, experiences a complete reversal of what just happened to ghrelin whilst the body is deep in ketosis. Typically, as you lose weight, cholecystokinin production decreases in a bid to induce you to eat more. However, ketosis prevents the levels from dropping even when the body is experiencing weight loss. This works out very well for anyone who is on the keto diet because we get spared the hunger pangs that usually accompany traditional dieting.

Some have actually asked if this would mean that the body may potentially waste itself into nothingness since feelings of hunger are suppressed and we may not know if we are truly hungry. To answer this, we would first have to come to an understanding that the body, as an organism, is a wonderful, intricately balanced piece of self-learning machine. The ability for the body to sort itself out is virtually second to none.

When we are in ketosis, we will still experience hunger as our energy stores run down through expenditure via daily activities. These feelings of hunger are what I would consider as true hunger, as they are not created from a carb induced state of affairs. When you feel such hunger on the ketogenic diet, it is usually a very strong signal to get your next meal! At least that is what I always do. That is why many keto practitioners always talk about eating only when you truly feel hungry and not be subjected to the usual social norms of eating during breakfast, lunch and dinner times. It really can feel quite liberating to be in touch with your body's needs. So the idea that we would gradually waste away to nothingness really does not hold much water because we still would get signals of hunger to prompt us to eat.

What really happens is that we get these hunger pangs less frequently than if we were to be still on a carb based diet. The adjustments in the produced levels of hunger controlling hormones do play their part, as do the satiating feeling of fats and proteins. There is also another reason for the less frequent hunger pangs. We simply are getting more energy from the fat burning!

More Energy and Mental Clarity

I am quite sure that I am not alone in having the experience of feeling weariness or even bone tired fatigue just after a meal heavy in carbs. Just imagine having had a hearty meal, perhaps even topping it off with a nice, sugary dessert, and literally within the hour you find yourself nodding off, scarcely able to keep your eyes open despite your best efforts. I know my many instances of bruised thighs can attest to how hard I pinch myself trying to keep awake.

The thing here with this fatigue is that it can be easily avoided, if you were to cut down on carbs! When the body breaks down carbs for fuel, the glucose generated needs insulin to act as a mediator in order to be transported into the various organs and cells to be used as energy. That is primarily the reason why our pancreas jacks up our insulin production whenever we have a carb heavy meal. The body knows that it needs to safely usher the blood sugar present in our bloodstream to be used as energy or to be converted and stored as fats.

In cases where our bodies are fairly young and not metabolically damaged, the resulting insulin sensitivity is still high and the pancreas is able to create just about the right amount of insulin to

17

match the level of blood sugar present. However, as we age and damage our bodies metabolically through inattention and diet, our insulin sensitivity decreases and this leads the pancreas to produce ever increasing amounts of insulin in order to ferry the same amount of blood sugar. The poor pancreas realizes that the body's cells aren't responding like they are previously to insulin and hence increases its production as the way to normalize the situation. This then results in a swift reduction of glucose in the blood stream which triggers the tiredness. If we give in to the fatigue and quickly go to bed, you might realize that we often wake up with a roaring hunger, which is also coupled with a strange feeling of bloated-ness in the stomach.

When there is low blood sugar in our bodies, the body triggers hunger signals in order to get additional fuel. The bloated feeling in the stomach though, is a result of food not being fully digested. If we think about it, a hearty lunch should let us feel satisfied all the way til dinner time in normal circumstances. Why is it that we get feelings of hunger and fatigue just a few hours after our last meal?

The key lies in the fuel that powers our body. Glucose triggers the insulin response, which in turn has the potential to create the so-called sugar crash that causes the tiredness and accompanying hunger. Energy based from sugar or glucose can be compared to a candle's light, flickering and winking, subject to the whims of the wind. When your body is energized by ketones however, this power source is akin to an electric bulb, shining bright steadily and consistently.

When our bodies burn fat, insulin is hardly called into action. This limits the sugar crash possibility. Also, as fat is easier to store and more readily available than glucose in our body, the ketones produced from fat can readily draw upon our body's fat stores. We get a stable source of fuel as a result, which then explains why we feel more energetic on the keto diet as compared to a regular one.

Ketones also provide more bang for the proverbial buck as compared to glucose, as they burn cleaner metabolically. When you place a plentiful source of fuel and couple it with the fuel's better energy giving capabilities, is it any wonder that you probably would feel like being able to handle all the work and house chores, and still have energy for that special project which you have always been wanting to embark on?

The buck doesn't stop here though. You may think having increased energy from the keto diet is really a great benefit. How about getting improved mental clarity to boot? Say goodbye to those days of fuzzy headedness and times when you just cannot seem to concentrate and be ready to embrace life with razor sharp mental alertness.

What really happens behind the scenes to account for the boosted mental acuity, is the effect of ketones on the brain. Our brain hangs on the balance of two major neurotransmitters, glutamate as well as gamma aminobutyric acid or otherwise known as GABA. Glutamate serves as a stimulant and is usually associated with intelligent processes, like talking or thinking abstractly. Geniuses are found to have higher levels of glutamate. Too high a level, without the balancing effect of GABA, would result in over stimulation of the brain. This is when seizures, strokes and generic neurodegeneration occurs. As it turns out, glutamate needs the presence of the calming GABA in order to head off the potentially debilitating effects of over stimulation.

What ketones does for the brain is to provide a more efficient way for which glutamate is processed into GABA, which then leads to a neural environment that has less neurons firing all at the same time. This translates to a real world effect of having better mental clarity and doing away with brain fog. The brain also appreciates ketones as a better fuel. While it has to be said that it does require some amount of glucose to maintain a healthy function, this amount of glucose can be easily provided for via the limited carbs we take in as well as the process of gluconeogenesis, which is the creation of glucose via proteins. The difference between glucose and ketones as fuel can be markedly attributed to their oxidative footprint. Glucose, in excess, induces far more oxidative stress than ketones. Factor in the fact that the brain is literally a glucose hog while we are off the keto diet, and you have a case where it is a matter of when, not if oxidative damage would harm the brain. With the presence of ketones however, this oxidative damage is somewhat curbed and sometimes even reversed, leading to postulations about the neuroprotective qualities of ketosis.

Boosted Brain Health with Keto

You might have encountered instances where you have read about how the ketogenic diet was used since the 1920s to help treat folks with epilepsy. It has been shown to reduce the incidence of seizures without the need for medication. In fact, treatment of epilepsy through dieting has long been espoused by the ancient Greeks. Hippocrates, the famous physician, was one of the forerunners of this therapy where medicine played a decidedly secondary role.

Various research and anecdotal evidence have pointed to the efficacy of the ketogenic diet in reducing or even totally suppressing seizures, particular in cases of childhood epilepsy. Recent medical research has postulated that the reason for these apparent benefits is mainly due to the increased energy production in the hippocampus, brought on by the introduction of ketones as fuel for the brain. The increased energy levels found in the brain was thought to contribute significantly in ensuring more stability in neuron activity. The research also showed that the ketogenic diet actually improved the brain's oxidative stress resistance, which bodes really well for other neurodegenerative diseases like Alzheimer's and Parkinson's.

Alzheimer's disease has been dubbed the diabetes of the brain, because the brain cells become insulin resistant and hence aren't able to receive their required amount of glucose. This deprivation of blood sugar to a glucose hog like the brain essentially means that much needed fuel for neural processes are lowered, sometimes too much, and it leads to neural system damage. This then paves the way for Alzheimer's to take root. With the brain fueled by ketones however, insulin resistance of the cells can effectively remedied, because there is very little need for insulin without reliance on glucose as fuel. Ketones also seem to provide an added layer of protection against oxidative damage.

For diseases like Parkinson's and certain types of dementia, oxidative damage to the brain cells, coupled with a lowered neural energy production, are thought to be the main culprits in letting these diseases take hold. When your body is in ketosis however, these two damaging factors are put on hold due to the presence of ketones.

Another thing to consider is the impact of the additional fat that the ketogenic diet introduces on the brain. The brain is effectively made up of about sixty percent fat. Polyunsaturated fats like the omega-3 fatty acids have been researched to show that they elicit positive reactions in the brain when introduced. In some cases of brain trauma, eicosapentaenoic acid or EPA, a form of omega-3 fatty acid, have been directly fed in via the intravenous system, and recovery times have been shown to be cut in half or more. EPA actually helps out with reducing the inflammatory damage wrought on the brain, either via trauma or from an erstwhile high carb diet. With the high fat keto diet in play, it would be natural to presume we would be getting more of these beneficial fats into our body system, thereby leading to better protection against neurodegeneration.

Though modern medical practice has yet to fully embrace the ketogenic diet and deploy it officially against neurodegenerative diseases, there has been no lack of scientific research and patient group studies which have pointed to the positive effects the diet has had in curbing and suppressing these diseases. I have no doubt that there would come a day when we can approach any doctor and talk freely about the keto diet. Right now though, I would strongly suggest filtering through the doctors to find those who actually know what the ketogenic diet is, and avoid the ones who just dismiss and scoff at the mere mention of it. This is for the benefit of your own health after all!

Reduced Inflammation with Keto

When we broach this topic, I reckon it might be good to delve a little deeper into what inflammation really is and how it impacts our body. Most of us would be quite familiar with what is known as acute inflammation. It sounds really bad, but really it is just the body's response to anything from a small cut on your finger to the nasty cold that somehow found its way into your system.

Basically the body senses that there are foreign pathogens or entities which are harmful and quickly dispatches the white blood cells to head off the threat. Various pro inflammatory gene expressions are also triggered in a bid to squash out these offending marauders. Make no mistake, inflammation is very much essential to human survival. Without it, I very much doubt we can survive the common cold because we would have no means with which to beat off the virus!

The tricky bit comes when we talk about chronic inflammation. Rheumatoid arthritis, asthma and the buildup of heart threatening arterial plaque are all instances of chronic inflammation at work. What usually happens is that the body is constantly exposed to agents or substances which it deems as a danger, hence the pro inflammatory responses are frequently being triggered. Over time, the body is constantly in a state of war and aggression, which is not very good news because everything needs balance.

On a carb based diet, sugar is the culprit that triggers inflammation. So imagine you are on the usual diet that is predominantly high in carbs, you are actually introducing pro inflammatory substances on a daily basis! Further to that, the additional oxidation on the cells caused by the presence of glucose also promotes inflammation.

As we switch over to the state of ketosis, certain anti-inflammatory responses come into play. Oxidative damage to the cells is reduced for one, as they utilize the cleaner ketones as fuel instead of glucose. This produces lesser reactive oxygen species or ROS, which is known to promote inflammation. Certain gene expressions that are known to be associated with increased inflammation are also muted due to the presence of increased fatty acid levels, particularly the polyunsaturated fatty acids. Also, whilst on the ketogenic diet, the chemical adenosine is known to have elevated production. This is great for anti-inflammatory purposes as adenosine acts to fight against inflammation and is a natural pain reliever.

Patients suffering from multiple sclerosis as well as non-alcoholic fatty liver disease, ailments which can trace their roots to chronic inflammation, have all reported doing better after just six to eight weeks on the ketogenic diet. The diet is also great for exercise recovery, as the anti-inflammatory conditions take hold in the body and decreases oxidative stress that exercise normally brings. One thing to note here is the potential for getting in some carbs just an hour or less before going for your exercise regime. When we are talking about getting in carbs before exercise, it should be noted that this is after your body has acclimated fully to the keto diet, which probably will be anything between three to six weeks. What I take is usually about 20g carbs, which translates to a banana or two, depending on the size, or maybe a bar of dairy chocolate. This spurt of energy helps especially if the exercise involves weight training or impact sports, where the body is called upon to exert itself in quick bursts. Normally we rely on glycogen for these quick bursts, but on the keto diet, glycogen would be non-existent. This is just something for you to think about and not an iron clad rule that must be followed, and as always, when in doubt, listen to your body. That will never fail you.

When you slow down inflammation and create a body environment that has a slight anti-inflammatory tilt, you also create a situation where the oxidative effects of aging are retarded to a certain degree. To put things simply, aging is the oxidation of our body. With the ketogenic diet reducing the impact that oxidative stress wrecks on our system, it would stand to reason that we could potentially slow premature aging which is caused by chronic inflammation. It might seem far-fetched to think that someday the keto diet could be the basis for which treatments are derived to reverse aging, but hey, one can always dream right?

Keto Control Of Diabetes

With diabetes being one of the major ailments sweeping the planet and claiming more and more patients, it is probably good news that we have a means with which to control it. Diabetes predominantly has two types. Let's talk about type 2 diabetes and how it is positively impacted by the keto diet.

Type 2 diabetes has its cause in the gradual erosion of insulin sensitivity across all the cells in the body. Our cells need insulin in order be able to use glucose for energy or to be stored as fat. Without the required amount of insulin, glucose would be stuck in the blood stream with nowhere to go. This leads to abnormal levels of blood sugar which is definitely not good news due to the pro inflammation qualities sugar has. When our cells become less and less insulin sensitive, the pancreas is forced to produce more and more insulin in order to induce the cells to be able to take up the glucose flooding in from the carb rich foods. The pancreas, however, cannot keep up the elevated insulin production indefinitely. There comes a point when the cells become so insulin desensitized that there will always be an elevated amount of blood sugar floating around the body despite the copious amounts of insulin being produced. Constantly having elevated blood sugar would mean diabetes of the type 2 variety has finally gotten a hold on the body. No need for tears yet though, because help is just around the corner!

Although the traditional diet mooted to treat diabetes has always been a variation of the low fat higher carb variety, with some going the distance to emphasize on the need for a low glycemic diet, a 24 week intervention study done in 2008 amongst others has shown that the low glycemic diet fared less favorably as compared to the ketogenic diet. The BMI, body weight as well as blood sugar levels all recorded greater percentage reductions for the folks who were on the 24 week keto diet.

The crux of the matter here is really about insulin. With a carb rich diet, despite it being lower on the glycemic index, glucose is still being introduced into the body as the main fuel. This means insulin is needed to ferry the glucose into cells for energy production. When we go into ketosis, fats replace carbs as the body's main fuel. Glucose in the blood stream becomes greatly reduced and so too is the reliance on insulin. Imagine your insulin desensitized cells as a boxer who is constantly being pummeled, on the same spot! This is what happens when glucose is still being used as the primary fuel for diabetics. Switch over to fat fueled ketones, and the pummeled boxer suddenly can get to his feet again without suffering from a rain of blows. In fact, there is a total cessation of hits on our erstwhile punched-up boxer, and he can take this time to recover. The same holds true for folks with type 2 diabetes. With the keto diet, it is not only a means with which the disease can be suppressed, it could possibly be used to reverse the insulin resistance of the body's cells. When you have a diet that can help to normalize blood sugar levels as well as reduce the need for insulin, it is not hard to see why there might be a chance to reverse the metabolic damage that was wrought by a carb rich diet.

For type 1 diabetes, it is a situation where the pancreas just cannot produce any insulin. That is the reason why folks with type 1 diabetes have got to rely on insulin shots in order to get energy into their cells after meals. The more carbs there is present in their meals, the more glucose it generates and the more insulin is correspondingly needed. With the keto diet, the insulin requirement would no doubt be drastically reduced due to the relative absence of glucose.

Some folks may take this opportunity to bring up ketoacidosis, a term that is continually linked to type 1 diabetic keto dieters. Ketoacidosis is a situation where there is a high level of ketones present in the blood, together with an elevated level of glucose. This potent mix can potentially cause feelings of nausea, giddiness and even death if left untreated. There is some concern that with the lack of insulin being produced by type 1 diabetics, there is a clear and present danger of having this deadly cocktail of elevated ketones as well as glucose for those who embark on the keto journey.

For me, I would always say go with the choice that is the most comfortable for yourself. However, do make sure that it is an informed decision. In order for ketoacidosis to happen, ketone levels have to be high, not the normal levels which you would commonly associate with nutritional ketosis. Besides, there is a need for the presence of high levels of blood sugar. On a keto diet, that should be something of a rarity, unless there is a loss of control and a carb binge occurs.

To me, type 1 diabetics can indeed still benefit from the ketogenic diet. They just have to be more careful and watch their carb intake like a hawk.

Metabolic Syndrome Brought To Heel

Called Syndrome X or insulin resistance syndrome, the metabolic syndrome is not really a particular sickness but rather a set of symptoms that points to a heightened risk of cardiovascular disease and other ailments.

The common understanding is that if you fulfil three of the five symptoms, then a metabolic syndrome diagnosis can be confirmed. Low HDL cholesterol readings, a high read out on blood sugar, blood triglyceride and blood pressure levels, together with a large waist line make up the famous five symptoms.

How the ketogenic diet helps is actually to reverse what you see above. What is low gradually becomes higher, and what is high eventually comes down back to the normal range. Folks on the keto diet can expect to see higher, more favorable HDL cholesterol levels after a sustained period of dieting. The corresponding triglyceride and blood sugar levels should normalize out and that comes as no surprise, since a high carb diet is the predominant contributor to a higher triglyceride and glucose reading. Weight loss, as we previously mentioned, normally follows on the keto diet. All these point very favorably to the reversal of the metabolic syndrome.

Another thing of note is that the LDL and total cholesterol levels would also see a corresponding decrease after the keto diet is allowed time to work its magic. You see, cholesterol is actually needed by our bodies to repair itself and is a substance that is essential to human life. We need cholesterol around in our bodies and having too little cholesterol is actually classified as a life threatening condition in the medical world. When we embark on the keto diet, our inflammation and oxidation levels should decrease, and couple this with the carb restriction, should see lesser need for the body to constantly repair any damage, metabolically inflicted or otherwise. This would also mean a lesser need for cholesterol to be transported around our bodies and hence an accompanying drop in their levels.

There might be some concerns about increased cholesterol intake due to the nature of fatty foods that the ketogenic diet recommends. The truth is, our body creates about 75 to 80% of the cholesterol it needs in the liver, while the remaining are supplied by the ingestion of foods. Any excess cholesterol not needed by the body is passed out or recycled back into the liver. Our body most definitely does not waste any resource as we can see!

As we get the metabolic syndrome back under control, the risks for diseases like heart attacks, diabetes as well as polycystic ovary syndrome are all positively reduced. Can you imagine there would be a day where eating fat actually staves off heart disease? It is happening, and only on the ketogenic channel!

Potential Cancer Retardant

The basis for this theory is founded upon the fact that cancer cells are thought to be able to subsist and flourish wholly on glucose without any presence of oxygen. This view was expounded by the late Otto Warburg in 1931 and the findings were the subject of a Nobel Prize award.

The idea that cancer cells take to glucose like a duck gliding into water is certainly not outlandish. Glucose is routinely used in medical tests to ascertain the spread of the disease and research has shown that cancer cells do thrive on glucose. What happens then, when we swap glucose for ketones as fuel for the cells? The predominant thought is the cancer cells would really starve to death, since their source of glucose is cut off.

It was also thought that this starvation could actually be applied across the board to all kinds of cancers, and that the corresponding tumors would respond alike to the keto diet and just shrink to nothingness.

Now it seems that it is not just so clear cut as we thought. It appears that different kinds of cancer may respond differently to the keto diet. Cancers of the brain seem to react more favorably to glucose deprivation, mainly because the tumors depend a lot on glucose for survival.

Colorectal cancer, it seems, also responds fairly well when there is sugar deprivation. Other cancers, like those of the breast do not show the same positive reaction.

However, what is fairly certain is the relationship between overall plasma glucose levels, insulin and the rate of proliferation of cancer cells. The lower we can drive plasma glucose and insulin, the slower the development of the cancer.

It is in this aspect that the ketogenic diet comes to its own. Insulin and blood sugar levels are almost always normalized when on the diet, which should bode well for anyone who is exploring alternatives to treat cancer.

Also, it is fairly well documented that cancers respond positively to the effects of fasting. On a typical fast that lasts a whole day, cancer cells are shown to have retarded their development and some have even died off. This clearly marks out fasting as one potent weapon to be utilized in the fight against cancer. However, many patients, already weak with side effects from the radiation or chemotherapy treatments, simply cannot see themselves going through a fast.

With the ketogenic diet on their side however, I would dare say they would be better equipped to go through the fast with lesser trepidation. Hunger suppression and appetite management have always been the hallmarks of the keto diet, and I should think these factors would stand them in good stead when folks suffering from cancer embark on the fast.

How Does Ketosis Help with Fasting?

The ketogenic diet is a powerful tool for weight loss and fat burn, but it can also be combined with fasting to maximize your benefits. Intermittent fasting, or IF, is a relatively new diet trend with ancient therapeutic roots and powerful benefits for weight loss and health. It simply involves alternating between periods of eating normally and eating a reduced calorie content or no food at all.

When it comes to intermittent fasting, there are several approaches to consider:

- **Skipping meals** – You can skip a certain meal once a day to lengthen your daily period of fasting (it works best if you skip breakfast or dinner).
- **Eating windows** – You can condense your food intake to a 4 to 7 hour window once a day, fasting for the remainder of the day.
- **Prolonged fast** – You can engage in an extended fasting period of 24 to 48 hours once a week or once a month.

The type of intermittent fasting you choose should be determined by your goals. When it comes to the benefits of intermittent fasting, there are many. Here are a few:

- Improved mental clarity
- Reduced fatigue and brain fog
- Increased energy levels
- Improved muscle growth and recovery
- Increased nutrient absorption
- Fewer side effects from cancer therapy

If you want to give intermittent fasting a try, one option is to use it to kick start your ketogenic diet with a 3-day cycle. Choose a day to start and eat a ketogenic meal at dinner time and make it your last meal of the day. The next morning, go for a brisk walk for at least an hour to use up your glycogen stores – be sure to stay hydrated. As an alternative, you can do a 30 to 45 minute HIIT (high intensity interval training) workout. For the rest of the day, taken an MCT oil supplement two or three times to keep your energy up.

The next day, test your ketones with a pin prick of your finger when you wake up – they should be somewhere around 0.7mmol or higher. (millimoles per liter, practitioners use it as a measure of blood ketone levels) If they are at that level or higher, keep going with your fast. If you are under that level, get some additional exercise and then test again. For the rest of the day and the following day, keep supplementing with MCT oil and incorporate some salts to keep your fluid levels balanced. On the evening of the third day, break your fast at dinner time with a ketogenic meal. At that point, you can continue with the 21-day meal plan provided later in this book.

Before you jump into the ketogenic diet, take a moment to learn about some of the precautions you might need to take with certain health problems. This diet is pretty much suitable for most folks, but there are certain health conditions which may make it trickier to go keto.

Is the Ketogenic Diet Suitable for Everyone?

By now the ketogenic diet probably sounds like a great idea, and it is! Unfortunately, this kind of diet is not recommended for everyone and you should check with your doctor to make sure it's safe before you make the switch. Be sure to check with a doctor who is familiar with what the ketogenic diet is, because there is a chance you may just get a negative response to keto when it could have been a green light for you.

The ketogenic diet is great for most individuals, but it could be dangerous for people with porphyria, Pyruvate Carboxylase Deficiency, or various metabolic disorders that tamper with the proper function of the liver. These conditions are somewhat rare, so you probably don't need to worry about them. There are, however, other specific situations which may require an extra level of care when following the ketogenic diet.

For example, if you have type 1 diabetes, you need to be careful when following a ketogenic diet due to the risk of ketoacidosis [11]. Ketoacidosis is a dangerous metabolic state in which the body is unable to produce enough insulin to normalize blood sugar levels. For type 1 diabetics, the carbs which they take in do not have the insulin to necessitate the conversion from glucose to energy. Hence, the body then produces ketones as a supplemental source of energy because it thinks there is a lack of glucose. In actuality, the glucose is stuck in the blood stream, unable to be utilized as fuel due to the absence of insulin. It is this mix of high blood sugar levels and ketones which gives ketoacidosis its dangerous edge. It should not, I have to emphasize this, be confused with ketosis, as was commonly done it the past. Ketoacidosis can only happen if the body has a distinct lack of insulin.

If left untreated, ketoacidosis can become fatal, so it is important to monitor your glucose and insulin levels closely if you have type 1 diabetes. As long as you continue to take supplemental insulin, the ketogenic diet can work for type 1 diabetics, but you need to take extra care in monitoring those levels.

Aside from people with diabetes, the ketogenic diet can have certain drawbacks for other individuals. For example, ketosis may have a negative impact for those with gallbladder issues, as a malfunctioning gallbladder would not have the ability to breakdown fats as it should. The standard ketogenic diet is also not recommended for people who do a great deal of high-intensity exercise because this form of body work requires quick-burning glucose for fuel. For these folks, there are variations which can be made to the ketogenic diet to cater to their specific needs.

The ketogenic diet is not without its fair share of thorns. There are some transient side effects which we will go through in the later chapter and I just want to say here that despite going through the somewhat unpleasant adjustments, I found it to be well worth it because of the benefits that the diet offers. Again, this isn't meant to be a pit stop pep talk, but an offering of my personal viewpoint that, whilst getting into ketosis isn't just plain easy sailing, those humps and bumps along the way will eventually become a hello to boosted energy and optimal fat burn!

Chapter 3
The Inner Sanctum: How Ketosis Works

The ketogenic diet is very easy in principle – simply structure your diet around healthy fats with moderate protein and low carbohydrate intake. The details are a little more complex, but that's about the size of it.

Having a basic understanding of the ketogenic diet and how it works, you are now ready to learn about the different variations of the ketogenic diet. There are three:

1. Standard Ketogenic Diet (SKD)
2. Targeted Ketogenic Diet (TKD)
3. Cyclical Ketogenic Diet (CKD)

The standard ketogenic diet is the most common and the rules are fairly easy to follow – just stick to the same minimal intake of net carbs all the time. If you are at all familiar with the Atkins Diet, the SKD is very similar to the Induction phase during which you consume no more than 20 to 50 grams of net carbs daily. In terms of macronutrient ratios, the SKD recommends 75% fat, 20% protein, and 5% carbohydrate. This version is the most common because once you get used to the formula, it becomes easy to follow and maintain.

The targeted ketogenic diet is a little more variable because you link your carb intake with your workout schedule. It is called "targeted" because you target your carbohydrates for your workout, consuming 25 to 50 grams of net carbs 30 to 60 minutes before you exercise. After working out, you should consume a recovery meal that is fairly high in protein in order to facilitate muscle repair and growth.

The TKD is popular among athletes and individuals who work out a lot because it ensures that you have enough fuel for your workout but also that you burn it off quickly, so it can't be stored as fat.

The cyclical ketogenic diet involves alternating between days of high carb consumption and low carb consumption. On your high-carb days you'll consume between 450 and 600 grams of carbohydrate over a 3- to 5-day period. On normal days, you'll consume about 50 grams of net carbs or less.

This type of ketogenic diet is popular among bodybuilders and athletes who want to maximize fat loss without sacrificing lean muscle mass. The CKD is definitely not for someone just starting out on the keto diet, stick to the standard version at the start and reap the rewards of ketosis!

In addition to these three types of ketogenic diet, there is a fourth – a restricted ketogenic diet for therapeutic use. This particular version is aimed at treating certain medical conditions such as cancer. When you reduce your carb intake to just 20 to 50 grams per day, your body will burn through its glycogen stores and begin producing ketone bodies – you know of this process as ketosis. In a state of ketosis, cancer cells will starve to death because they can only feed on glucose – healthy cells can survive on ketone bodies, so they won't be affected.

Combined with a calorie-restricted diet, research suggests that the ketogenic diet turns your body into an inhospitable environment for cancer cells. Other conditions for which the ketogenic diet may be beneficial include epilepsy, neurological diseases, depression, and migraines.

What is the Optimal Macronutrient Ratio?

Before you get started with the ketogenic diet, you should decide which version of the diet you want to follow. Once you've made that choice, you can start looking into the ideal macronutrient ratio. Your macronutrient ratio is simply the amount of carbohydrates, protein, and fats that you consume in relation to each other. Take the standard ketogenic diet for example – this diet recommends a macronutrient ratio of 75% fat, 20% protein, and 5% carbohydrate.

Depending on your goals, you can choose to stick with this standard macronutrient ratio or you can make adjustments. To calculate your personalized macronutrient range, you'll need to start by calculating your needs for each of the three macronutrients.

For carbohydrates, you'll be calculating your net carb intake – this simply means that you take the total number of carbs (in grams) and subtract the grams of fiber. A good range to aim for if you're just getting started with the ketogenic diet is 20g net carbs per day. Once you're in ketosis, you can play around with the numbers a little bit and can go as high as 30 or 40g net carbs per day. If you're going with the CKD or TKD, however, you'll have to factor in the additional carbs that you will be consuming depending on the cycle or workouts planned.

When it comes to protein, your needs depend on your goal. If your goal is to lose weight while preserving lean muscle mass, you should consume about 0.7 to 0.8 grams of protein per pound of lean body mass. Your lean body mass is simply your total bodyweight minus your body fat weight. You can use calipers to measure your body fat percentage or you can actually choose the easier route and use an Omron machine which passes a mild

36

electric current through your body to determine the body fat percentage. As an example, if you weigh 160 pounds and have 30% body fat, that would be about 48 pounds of fat. To preserve lean muscle mass, you would multiply your lean body mass (160 - 48 = 112) by 0.7 or 0.8 grams for a total of up to 90g protein per day. If you want to gain muscle mass, multiply it by 0.8 to 1.2 g per pound of lean body mass.

Fats are the most important macronutrient in the ketogenic diet and you should fill in the rest of your daily energy requirements with fat. To determine your specific needs, you'll want to start by calculating your daily energy needs. You'll learn more about how to do this in Chapter 5.

What Are the Best Fats for Ketosis?

By now you well know that the ketogenic diet is all about fat, but not all fats are created equal. Some fats are good for you and can boost your results with the ketogenic diet while others are very unhealthy and should be avoided.

For many years, people were led to believe that all saturated fats are bad. Now, however, the truth has become clear – some saturated fats are actually very good for you! In fact, some of the best saturated fats work well as a staple for cooking so you can use them freely. Here are some of the best fats to use in cooking for the ketogenic diet:

- Butter
- Ghee
- Lard
- Tallow
- Coconut Oil

Saturated fats are simply fats that are typically solid at room temperature. They are the most stable kind of fats from a chemical viewpoint. Stable is good for the body because the more stable the fat is, the less likely it is to suffer from oxidation. Oxidized anything is bad for our bodies. For example, think about an apple, cut open, with the soft white flesh exposed. Within hours, it turns brown due to oxidation. As long as I can remember, saturated fats have always been the bad boy around town and have been erroneously linked to heart disease. With the more recent research input actually exonerating saturated fats, I would say to please enjoy them with peace of mind. I know, years of conditioning, and what I believe to be wrong education, can make it hard at first, but take it a step at a time. Start off small and monitor your cholesterol levels if you are really worried. I think you'd would be hard pressed to find a more paranoid person than me when it comes to cholesterol levels, because I was having troubles with them due to the erstwhile high carb diet. But in all my paranoia, if I could take the plunge into saturated fats and come out unscathed, I have no doubt you can as well! Butter and coconut oil are the easiest cooking fats to come by, though you may be able to find ghee, tallow, or lard at your local grocery store.

The second group of fats that should be a staple of your ketogenic diet is monounsaturated fatty acids (MUFAs) Found primarily in avocado, beef, nuts, and olive oil, MUFAs are very good for your heart. Polyunsaturated fats like omega-3 fatty acids are also great for your heart and for your health in general. You can find these fats in foods like wild salmon, grass-fed meats, cod liver oil, walnuts, and macadamia nuts. The other well-known polyunsaturated fat would be the omega-6 acid. This is copiously present in our processed foods and we are usually taking in too much of it. Just make sure you get a healthy balance of both omega-3 and omega-6. A ratio of one part omega-3 to four parts omega-6 would be a good place to aim for. Eventually you should be gunning for an optimal ratio of one is to one. At least that should be the target!

Another group of fats you should include in your diet would be medium-chain triglycerides, or MCTs. This type of fat is very easy for the body to digest which makes it a great source of immediate energy. Examples of foods that are rich in MCTs include coconut oil, butter, and palm oil. In addition to using these fats in recipes, you can also purchase MCT oil in supplement form. Shoot for the ones with more caprylic as well as capric acids. MCTs are great for that added energy boost, as well as kick starting the body's natural ketogenic response.

Now, what about unhealthy fats that you should avoid? All processed and hydrogenated oils are best avoided – this includes margarine, hydrogenated vegetable oil, and other trans fats. You should also steer clear of sunflower, safflower, canola, cottonseed, grapeseed, and corn oils. Most trans fats that we see in the market today actually originated from chemical processes, which is why they are sometimes known as franken-fats. There are natural trans fats, but their amounts are so infinitesimal that we do not really have to worry about them. The real danger is with the artificially produced ones. If you have to avoid any fats, be sure to make trans fats your top target

What About Protein Intake?

While fat is the star of the ketogenic diet, protein is important as well. Not only does it help you to maintain lean muscle mass, it is important for weight loss and overall health and wellness. The ketogenic diet is by no means a high-protein diet, but you should get about 20% of your daily calories from protein.

But how is protein so important for weight loss?

Scientific studies show that protein offers the most satiating effect as a macronutrient while carbs have the least. This means that eating a protein-rich food will keep you feeling full for longer than a carb-heavy food. Protein also increases energy expenditure due to a concept called the Thermic Effect of Food (TEF). This simply refers to the amount of energy it takes to digest and metabolize protein – it is estimated at 20% to 30%. So, if you consume 100 calories of protein, you'll really only be absorbing about 70 because it takes about 30 calories to digest it [12].

Another important benefit of protein for weight loss is that it preserves and builds muscle tissue. As you may or may not know, muscle burns more calories at rest than fat. This means that you can boost your metabolism simply by building more muscle. It may only be about 100 calories a day, but every bit counts!

So, how much protein do you actually need and how is it determined?

The amount of protein you need in your daily diet will be determined by your bodyweight and your activity level. The more active you are, the higher your protein needs will be. As mentioned in an earlier section, you can calculate your protein needs by using your lean body mass – your total body weight minus your body fat. Other factors like gender and age may play a role as well, but less so. You'll learn how to calculate your exact needs in Chapter 5.

Though protein is important on the ketogenic diet, you want to be careful about eating too much. If you consume too much protein, your body will produce a hormone called glucagon which will convert the protein into glucose via a process known as gluconeogenesis.

With low carbohydrate intake, gluconeogenesis helps to protect you from low blood sugar but if you eat too much protein gluconeogenesis could get in the way of achieving a state of ketosis.

How Many Carbs Can You Eat?

You've already learned about some of the negative effects of the typical Western diet, but just how bad is a lifetime of carb consumption for your body?

The main problem with excess carb consumption is that it causes your blood sugar level to rise. If you are consistently eating a lot of carbs, your blood sugar might remain higher than the normal level which can lead to all kinds of damage. Most significantly, it can lead to type 2 diabetes.

When you consume food, your body immediately begins working to break it down. Enzymes in your saliva and acids in your stomach break the food down into its core components, the most important of which is glucose. As the glucose hits your blood stream, your pancreas receives a signal to start producing a hormone called insulin. As the insulin in your blood rises, your cells and tissues are able to absorb the glucose and can utilize it for energy.

The problem occurs when your blood sugar remains persistently high. If you keep eating high-carb foods, your body will have to produce more insulin just to achieve the same effect. Over time, your body may become less sensitive to insulin – this is called insulin resistance and it is a hallmark of type 2 diabetes. But what exactly does chronic high blood sugar levels do?

Here are some of the complications associated with chronic hyperglycemia [13]:

- Inflammation that contributes to chronic disease
- Increased risk for heart attack and stroke
- Peripheral artery disease
- Poor kidney function, eventual kidney failure
- Nerve damage that can lead to loss of sensation
- Eye diseases such as glaucoma and cataracts
- Periodontal disease and other dental problems

In addition to these health problems, high blood sugar can combine with other conditions such as high blood pressure, high cholesterol, and obesity to form what is known as the metabolic syndrome. Having metabolic syndrome may or may not produce symptoms but it can increase your risk for other serious health problems such as diabetes and cardiovascular disease [14].

Reducing your carb intake by switching to the ketogenic diet may help to repair some of the problems caused by long-term carb consumption. You still need to eat some carbs, as was mentioned earlier, but you should limit your intake. When you are first starting out on the ketogenic diet, you may want to start with around 50 to 60g net carbs per day while you make the transition and then lower it to 20 to 30g per day gradually in order to ensure you enter a state of ketosis.

Or you could just bite the bullet and drop straight to 20g net carbs per day at the start to ensure you hit ketosis. That was how I did it.

If you want to determine your individual carb limit, you'll need to invest in some testing supplies. Once you determine that your body is in ketosis, you can start adding more net carbs to your diet – about 5g per week. Keep adding carbs until you detect a very low level of ketones or none at all.

When that happens, you've reached your carb limit and you can use that information going forward. If you choose to follow the cyclic ketogenic diet or the targeted ketogenic diet, you will have to adjust your carb intake according to your workout habits.

What Should You Expect Getting Started?

If you've done any research about the ketogenic diet before, you may be familiar with the term "keto flu". This term simply refers to the collection of symptoms you might experience as your body transitions from burning carbohydrates to burning fat for fuel. Some of the most common symptoms of keto flu include the following [15]:

- Low energy levels
- Brain fog
- Increased hunger/cravings
- Problems with sleep
- Nausea or upset stomach
- Bad breath
- Leg cramps or soreness
- Changes in bowel habits
- Electrolyte imbalance
- Headaches or migraines

Though the transition into ketosis may come with some unpleasant side effects, you should know that it can happen with any diet. Making significant changes to your diet comes with a risk for digestive upset, low energy, and other issues that will sort themselves out eventually. I cannot stress enough that while these side effects might very well be somewhat hindering, and in some cases downright irritating, I can assure you that many find that the cure to all of these hindrances actually lies in getting sufficient rest as well as ensuring you are well hydrated. We shall be touching on these pesky side effects again later when talking about troubleshooting, and we will talk more about specific solutions.

Once you've made it through the transition and have entered ketosis, you have some wonderful things to look forward to! In addition to kick starting your weight loss, entering ketosis comes with a boost of natural energy and renewed confidence and motivation to stick to the diet. You'll also find that you feel less hungry between meals and that you are better able to concentrate. You may also notice that your mood swings stabilize and you feel more positive in general.

How Do You Know When You're in Ketosis?

You can decrease your carbohydrate intake and increase your fat intake and still not reap the benefits of the ketogenic diet. Why? Because your body needs to be in a state of ketosis in order for you to benefit from it. In order to determine whether your body is in ketosis or not, there are three testing options:

- Breath analysis
- Urine analysis
- Blood analysis

The simplest method of testing for ketosis is testing your breath – if it smells fruity or metallic, it could be an indication of ketosis. You can also purchase breath-ketone analyzers, but they can be fairly expensive, and generally cost upwards of $150. This testing method is easy, you just have to exhale normally into the breath analyzer for about 5 to 10 seconds. The idea is to expel most of the air from the lungs in order to get a more accurate test. The issue with this method is that sometimes the analyzers malfunction, and you cannot get an accurate reading of your ketone levels like you would with ketone blood testing.

To test for ketosis using urine analysis, you'll need to purchase testing strips. Simply hold the test end of the strip under your urine stream, shake off excess liquid, and wait for 15 seconds. If you have successfully entered ketosis, the test strip will change from beige to purple – the deeper the purple, the higher the ketone levels in your blood. Keep in mind that darker is not necessarily better – your perfect level of ketosis will be unique to you. One thing about urine testing is that you may be testing positive for ketones one day, and then find that the ketones disappear from the urine some days later. There are two explanations for this. The first would be you got knocked out of ketosis, probably by consuming too many carbs. It's fine, get back on the keto wagon again and continue the fat burning journey. The second is that your body is still in ketosis, but the ketones are not appearing in your urine purely because it is being utilized as fuel in your body. If you find yourself still having higher energy levels and better mental clarity despite no ketones in the urine, chances are you have nothing to worry about!

Though a urine test is a simple way to test for ketones, it isn't as accurate as a blood test. For one thing, your level of hydration can dilute the ketones in your urine which may result in a false negative test. To use a blood test, you need to prick your finger then smear the blood on a test strip and insert it into a blood ketone monitor. Consider the options and then choose the testing method you think suits you best.

For me, I tend to go with the blood ketone testing when I start the keto diet. It gives me accurate number readings of my blood ketone levels and at the same time, those numbers serve to motivate me as well, telling me that I am on the right path.

The normal range for blood ketone levels would be between 0.7 to 3 mmol when we are in nutritional ketosis, which is the state all of us are gunning for when we go on the ketogenic diet. After I am keto adapted, which usually takes about 3 to 6 weeks for me, I then switch over to using the breath analyzer, just to be certain that I am still in ketosis. The logic here is that, after your body is keto adapted and knows to burn fat for fuel, this would usually remain the status quo until something comes along to upset the balance – that is why we use the breath analyzer to confirm that our bodies are still producing ketones but we do not need the exact values. This lowers cost because blood testing is still the most expensive method out there.

Now that you know what to expect as you move forward with the ketogenic diet, you're ready to get into the specifics. In the next chapter, we'll talk about the foods you can and cannot eat on the ketogenic diet before we get into the step-by-step guide.

Chapter 4
The Clean, The Dirty & The Staples:
Keto Food

When following the ketogenic diet, you will be eating a mixture of all three macronutrients – protein, fat, and carbohydrate. As you've already learned, however, you'll be eating more of some than others. In regard to the specific foods you'll be eating, some of the main food groups will be as follows:

- Healthy fats like olive oil, butter, coconut oil, nuts, and seeds
- Grass-fed meats and pasture-raised poultry
- Cage-free eggs and full-fat dairy products
- Wild-caught fish and seafood
- Non-starchy vegetables and some fruits

You can also enjoy coffee and herbal tea for beverages as well as both fresh and dried herbs and spices. Avoid fruit juice due to the high sugar and calorie content and try to include some bone broth for its probiotic benefits. You can continue to use some store-bought products like condiments and salad dressings, just be sure they don't contain a lot of added sugar or calories.

Ketogenic Diet Food List

Wondering exactly which foods are and are not included in the ketogenic diet? Here is a comprehensive ketogenic diet food list to get you started:

Foods to Eat Freely (Healthy Fats and Proteins)

- Avocado
- Butter
- Coconut milk
- Coconut oil
- Cocoa butter
- Olives
- Olive oil
- Avocado oil
- Macadamia oil
- MCT oil
- Lard
- Tallow
- Ghee
- Macadamia nuts
- Brazil nuts
- Pecans
- Nut butters
- Bacon
- Coconut shavings
- Eggs
- Beef
- Pork
- Lamb
- Organ meats
- Chicken
- Turkey
- Shellfish
- Catfish
- Cod
- Flounder
- Salmon
- Halibut
- Mackerel
- Mahi-Mahi
- Trout
- Tuna

Foods to Enjoy in Moderation (Full-Fat Dairy, Non-Starchy Veggies, Some Fruits)

- Cheese
- Heavy cream
- Yogurt
- Sour cream
- Mayonnaise
- Cottage cheese
- Cream cheese
- Walnuts
- Almonds
- Hazelnuts
- Peanuts
- Pine nuts
- Chia seeds
- Flaxseed
- Coconut flour
- Almond flour
- Unsweetened coconut
- Broccoli
- Cauliflower
- Green beans
- Bell peppers
- Mushrooms
- Spinach
- Lettuce

- Kale
- Cabbage
- Onions
- Garlic
- Raspberries

- Blackberries
- Blueberries
- Lemon
- Lime
- Nut flours

Foods to Avoid

- All-purpose flour
- Baking mix
- Whole-wheat flour
- Pastry flour
- Cake flour
- Cereal
- Pasta
- Rice
- Corn
- Baked goods
- Corn syrup
- Cereal bars
- Snack bars
- Quinoa
- Buckwheat
- Barley
- Couscous
- Oats
- Muesli
- Margarine
- Canola oil
- Hydrogenated oils
- Apples

- Bananas
- Mangos
- Melon
- Pineapple
- Potatoes
- Sweet potatoes
- Candy
- Dairy chocolate
- Ice cream
- Sports drinks
- Juice cocktail
- Soda
- Beer
- Low-fat foods
- Diet foods
- Low-fat dairy
- Artificial sweeteners
- White sugar
- Brown sugar
- Maple syrup
- Honey
- Agave

As previously mentioned, you can still use store-bought condiments like ketchup as long as you choose reduced sugar options. Mustard, mayonnaise, soy sauce, and Sriracha are fine in small amounts as are oil-based salad dressings and vinaigrettes. You can use horseradish, Worcestershire, and hot sauce in moderation. Fresh and dried herbs and spices are fine for unlimited use.

What About Alcohol and Sweeteners?

When following the ketogenic diet, you are free to consume high-fat foods, but that doesn't mean you can load up on candy and sweets – these foods are high in carbohydrates and unhealthy sweeteners. If you must sweeten something, choose a natural sweetener that is low in both calories and carbs – some popular options include the following:

- Powdered erythritol
- Liquid stevia extract
- Monk fruit

You may also be able to find sugar-free flavored syrups for dishes like pancakes, but be mindful of the ingredients and sweeteners. As is true for any diet, you should moderate your intake of sweeteners on the ketogenic diet and when you do enjoy sweeteners, choose from the list above.

Now, what about alcohol? Beer is best avoided on the ketogenic diet because it is high in carbs. If you choose to drink, opt for hard liquor over beer and mixed drinks. The best liquors to choose are vodka, tequila, gin, whiskey, rum, scotch, brandy, and cognac. Enjoy these liquors on the rocks (with ice) or with tonic water. Watch out for flavored alcohols like coconut rum or peach schnapps as well as sugary mixers like triple sec, sour mix, grenadine, and margarita mix.

If you prefer wine, keep in mind that the carb and calorie count will vary widely from one bottle to another. For red wines, cabernet sauvignon, pinot noir, and merlot are the best. For white wine, choose pinot grigio, sauvignon blanc, chardonnay or champagne. Just be on the lookout for very sweet wines like moscato, zinfandel, and dessert wines. You may also be able to enjoy light beers if it fits within your daily carb count – these beers usually range from 2 to 6.5g net carbs.

Keto Staple Foods

Though you've already received a comprehensive list of keto-friendly foods, there are certain "staples" you should focus on. Here is a quick list of ketogenic staple foods to include in your diet:

- Coconut
- Coconut butter
- Dark cacao butter
- Coconut oil
- Coconut water
- Avocado
- Avocado oil
- Extra-virgin olive oil
- Eggs
- Grass-fed butter
- MCT oil
- Dark chocolate (>90%)

As you get into the recipes section of this book, you'll see that these are some of the foods featured most often. This group of food serves as an essential go-to list when you need that daily fat intake without having to think too much.

Things like simply consuming an avocado or two in the morning really boosts up the fat quota for the day – remember we need about 75% of our daily calories from fats whilst on the keto diet. Eggs as well as butter are great sources of fats and protein, while the coconut is simply the Swiss army knife equivalent of the keto food list.

Coconut oil can be used for cooking, or for simple consumption. Coconut butter as well as dried coconut flesh shavings are useful staples which do not require much preparation. Coconut water, while not exactly low carb, will serve to provide a rich source of electrolytes that helps to balance the body's micronutrient needs – just make sure you do not take in more than one small cup daily, else you will bust your carb limit.

Don't worry if you've never used these foods before – I've provided instructions and you'll learn quickly!

Chapter 5
The Journey Begins With A Single Step: Keto Guide

At this point, you should have a thorough understanding of the ketogenic diet including what it is and how it works. You've received a wealth of information and helpful tips for following the diet, but now comes the hard part – actually doing it.

If you've tried other diets in the past, you may be a bit skeptical about how easy the ketogenic diet will be to follow. Any diet comes with its challenges, but the ketogenic diet offers a few benefits that make it easier to stick to:

- You don't have to severely restrict your calorie intake
- You get to eat plenty of high-fat foods
- You don't have to give up red meat and dairy products

Being able to keep eating some of your favorite foods is a major bonus for the ketogenic diet and will help sustain you through the hard times. It might be challenging at first to cut carbohydrates and to start eating more fat, but it is well worth it in the end. If you're ready to get started, keep reading for a step-by-step guide.

Phase 1 – It All Starts in the Mind

The biggest challenge for many people trying to start the keto diet is getting rid of the "fats are bad" mindset. You've probably had it drilled into your head that eating fatty foods is what makes you fat, but that simply isn't true – at least, it isn't quite that simple. Eating more calories than you burn is what makes you fat and the type of food you overindulge in affects how those excess calories are stored. Overeating carbohydrates can lead to weight gain just as easily as overeating fat.

In addition to giving up the notion that fat is bad, you also need to examine your motivation for switching to the ketogenic diet before you actually take the plunge. Do you want to lose weight? Do you want to improve your health? Do you want to prevent prediabetes from developing into full-blown diabetes?

There are many motivations for switching to the ketogenic diet and it is up to you to identify your motivations and to use them to keep going when the going gets tough.

Not only do you need to understand your own motivation for going keto, but you should be prepared to talk about your choice with other people. If your friends know that you're trying to lose weight and they see you chowing down on a ribeye steak, they are likely to ask questions. Prepare yourself with knowledge about the ketogenic diet so you can educate your friends and turn critics into a support system.

Phase 2 – Before You Go Keto

The next step in switching to the ketogenic diet is talking to your doctor. You've already read about some of the health conditions that may not mesh well with the ketogenic diet, but you should still ask your doctor if it is safe for you to make the switch. Even if you don't have any contraindicated health problems, you might want to ask about any medications you're taking just to be safe.

Once you have your doctor's permission to go ahead with the diet you need to do some math to determine your ideal macronutrient ratio and calorie intake.

Start by calculating your daily recommended calorie intake by using the Mifflin St. Joer equation [16]. Here's how it goes:

Men = 10 x weight (kg) + 6.25 x height (cm) – 5 x age (years) + 5

Women = 10 x weight (kg) + 6.25 x height (cm) – 5 x age (years) - 161

Using the appropriate equation above, plug in your numbers for weight, height, and age to find your Basal Metabolic Rate (BMR). Your BMR is the number of calories your body would burn in a day if you just sat on the couch all day – it is the minimum number of calories required to maintain essential biological processes.

Once you have your BMR you need to factor in your exercise to determine your total daily calorie expenditure. Choose the right factor and multiply it with your BMR:

- Sedentary (little to no exercise) = BMR x 1.2
- Lightly Active (light exercise 1-3 days/week) = BMR x 1.375
- Moderately Active (moderate exercise 3 -5 days/week) = BMR x 1.55
- Very Active (hard excrcisc 6-7 days/week) = BMR x 1.725
- Extra Active (very hard exercise & physical job or 2x daily training) = BMR x 1.9

After doing the math, you can then determine your ideal calorie intake. If you're trying to lose weight, you'll need to create a calorie deficit by subtracting from your total daily expenditure – a 10% to 20% reduction is recommended for weight loss.

Now that you have your daily calorie intake, you can figure out your ideal macronutrient ratio and the number of grams for each macronutrient. To give you an example of how it works, let's calculate the total daily energy needs of a 150-pound woman aged 45 with a height of 5'5" and a light activity level. (1 kg is approximately 2.2 pounds, 1 foot is approximately 30cm) Here's how to use the Mifflin St. Joer equation to find her BMR:

$BMR = (10 \times 68) + (6.25 \times 165) - (5 \times 45) - 161$

$BMR = 680 + 1{,}031 - 225 - 161$

$BMR = 1{,}325$

Now, if you factor in a light activity level, you would multiply the 1,325 by 1.375 for a daily energy expenditure of 1,821 calories. If this woman was trying to lose weight, she might factor in a 15% calorie reduction for a daily calorie goal of about 1,550 calories. Referring back to the earlier section of this book that covered macronutrient ratios, you can now calculate this woman's daily intake for fat, protein, and carbohydrate.

Let's start with fat. If you remember, the ideal fat intake for the standard ketogenic diet is about 75%. So, you would take 75% of the daily calorie intake (1,550) which gives you about 1,163 calories for fat. Keeping in mind that each gram of fat contains 9 calories, you are left with about 129 grams of fat.

Next, let's calculate protein. If you take 20% of the total calories each day, you'll get 310 calories – divide that by 4 calories per gram, which is the number of calories present in each gram of protein and you get about 78 grams protein. Finally, you're left with 5% carbohydrate, or about 78 calories. Divide it by 4 calories per gram, which also happens to be the amount found in each gram of carbohydrate and you get about 20 grams of carbohydrate. It's that easy!

Now that you have an example, you can apply these formulas to determine your own BMR, total daily expenditure, and daily calorie goal. Then, simply apply the 75/20/5 macronutrient ration to find out how many grams of fat, protein, and carbohydrate to consume each day. You can then use these numbers to create your own meal plans that will have your body switching over into ketosis in a matter of weeks.

If you need some help getting started, you'll be glad to know that I've included a 21-day meal plan with recipes in this book. It is based on a daily calorie goal of 2,000 calories, so you may need to make some adjustments depending on your calculations.

With your calculations completed, you are ready to get started with the ketogenic diet. Before you actually get going, however, there is some basic information that might help you. For example, you'll need to know how to read food labels to determine the fat, protein, and net carbs for certain products. The part of the food label you'll need to look at is the nutrition facts. You'll see the number of calories per serving listed as well as the number of calories from fat. You'll also find the grams per serving for fats, carbohydrates, protein, and fiber. To calculate net carbs, simply subtract the fiber content from the carb content. It might also help if you actually write down your personal macronutrient daily allotment somewhere where it is easily handy. As you start out, it would serve as a good reminder of your daily limits. The usual tricky bit is limiting the carbs, while trying to ensure you hit the fat content. Now you're ready to take the first step toward switching to the ketogenic diet!

Phase 3: Getting into the Food

With all of the background work completed, your next step is to clear your refrigerator and pantry of non-ketogenic foods. Depending on your current dietary habits, you might be left with an empty kitchen. Don't worry, though – the meal plan you're going to be following for the next three weeks comes with a shopping list so you can stock up on everything you're going to need!

Wondering what to do with all of that food you won't be eating?

If possible, try not to waste it. Ask your friends and family if they could use any of the food – especially fresh and frozen foods. For nonperishables, consider donating to a local food bank or shelter. If you have some moderate-carb foods, you might keep them for days that you work out, but you should plan to get rid of most of your high-carbohydrate foods.

In addition to cleaning out your pantry, you may want to take a look at the kitchen tools you have and consider whether you might need to buy some new ones. If you have a food processor or blender, you'll be able to make most of the recipes provided in this book with no problem. You'll also need a slow cooker, but you can purchase one for fairly cheap. Optional kitchen tools include a hand blender (also known as an immersion blender or stick blender) and a hand mixer or stand mixer.

Your 21-Day Meal Plan for Ketosis

Congratulations! You've finally made to the part where the fat's in the fire – The 21-day meal plan.

For the next three weeks, your entire diet is laid out for you in simple terms with quick and easy recipes. All you have to do is use the shopping lists to stock up on ingredients at the beginning of each week and then follow the meal plan!

If you take a quick look at the meal plan, you'll see that every day includes three meals plus one snack, dessert, or drink to enjoy at your discretion. You'll also find that each recipe lists the calories and macros and that each day has a total.

Remember, the meal plan is based on a 2,000-calorie daily intake (give or take 100 calories) and an approximate macronutrient ratio of 70% to 80% fat, about 10% to 20% protein, and 5% to 10% carbohydrates.

Without further ado, here are three 7-day meal plans to get you started!

Week 1 Meal Plan

Day	Breakfast	Lunch	Dinner	Snack/Dessert	Calories/Macros
1	Biscuits with Gravy and 1 Cup Avocado	Creamy Fish Chowder	Seared Salmon with Sautéed Kale	Guacamole Deviled Eggs & Coconut Chia Pudding	Calories: 1,970 Fat: 156 g Protein: 102.5 g Net Carbs: 29.5 g
2	Mexican-Style Scrambled Eggs with ½ Medium Avocado	Leftover Creamy Fish Chowder	Rosemary Apple Pork Tenderloin	Leftover Guacamole Deviled Eggs & Banana Lime Smoothie	Calories: 2,035 Fat: 157.5 g Protein: 118.5 g Net Carbs: 28 g
3	Leftover Biscuits with Gravy and 2 Slices Thick-Cut Bacon	Warm Zucchini Walnut Salad	Leftover Rosemary Apple Pork Tenderloin	Curry Spiced Almonds & Almond Cinnamon Bars	Calories: 1,995 Fat: 166 g Protein: 106.5 g Net Carbs: 21 g
4	Bacon-Wrapped Spinach Quiches with 4 Slices Thick-Cut Bacon	BLT Sandwich	Coconut Chicken Curry	Leftover Curry Spiced Almonds & Almond Cinnamon Bars	Calories: 1,995 Fat: 162 g Protein: 109.5 g Net Carbs: 27.5 g
5	Leftover Bacon-Wrapped Spinach Quiches with 1 Cup Avocado	Spinach and Steak Salad	Broccoli Cheddar Casserole with Lamb	Chia Peanut Butter Bites & Vanilla White Chocolate Fat Bombs	Calories: 1,920 Fat: 144.5 g Protein: 114.5 g Net Carbs: 24 g

Week 1 Meal Plan				
Day	**Breakfast**	**Lunch**	**Dinner**	**Snack/Dessert**	**Calories/Macros**
6	Breakfast Pizza Skillet	Leftover BLT Sandwich with ½ Medium Avocado	Pan-Seared Lemon Rosemary Chicken	Cheesy Sausage Dip & Sweet Cinnamon Bread	Calories: 2,030 Fat: 152 g Protein: 121.5 g Net Carbs: 31 g
7	Bacon Zucchini Hash with ½ Medium Avocado	Cheddar-Stuffed Burgers	Leftover Broccoli Cheddar Casserole with Lamb	Salted Kale Chips & Leftover Sweet Cinnamon Bread	Calories: 1,960 Fat: 151.5 g Protein: 114 g Net Carbs: 25.5 g

Week 2 Meal Plan

Day	Breakfast	Lunch	Dinner	Snack/Dessert	Calories/Macros
8	Breakfast Pockets	Easy Egg Salad with 1 Cup Avocado	Pork-Stuffed Zucchini Boats	Bacon Jalapeno Quick Bread & Strawberry Lemon Smoothie	Calories: 1,980 Fat: 157.5 g Protein: 102.5 g Net Carbs: 27.5 g
9	Cheddar Sausage Omelet	Creamy Cauliflower Soup	Broccoli White Fish Casserole	Leftover Bacon Jalapeno Quick Bread & Coconut Brownies	Calories: 1,940 Fat: 152.5 g Protein: 105.5 g Net Carbs: 29 g
10	Leftover Breakfast Pockets	Leftover Creamy Cauliflower Soup with ½ Medium Avocado	Leftover Broccoli White Fish Casserole	Almond Sesame Crackers & Blueberry Protein Smoothie	Calories: 1,950 Fat: 149 g Protein: 113 g Net Carbs: 31 g
11	Chocolate Mocha Chia Pudding and ½ Medium Avocado	Meaty Pizza Casserole	Ribeye Steak with Green Beans and ½ Medium Avocado	Cauliflower Cheese Dip & Leftover Coconut Brownies	Calories: 2,020 Fat: 163.5 g Protein: 99.5 g Net Carbs: 26.5 g
12	Chocolate Coconut Pancakes with ½ Medium Avocado	Spinach and Goat Cheese Pie	Leftover Ribeye Steak with Green Beans	Leftover Cauliflower Cheese Dip & Vanilla Almond Butter Smoothie	Calories: 1,975 Fat: 154 g Protein: 96 g Net Carbs: 27.5 g

Week 2 Meal Plan				
Day	**Breakfast**	**Lunch**	**Dinner**	**Snack/Dessert**	**Calories/Macros**
13	Leftover Chocolate Coconut Pancakes	Pork Egg Roll Bowl	Lamb Chops with Herb Butter	Creamsicle Fat Bombs & Lemon Poppy Ice Cream	Calories: 1,925 Fat: 152.5 g Protein: 98 g Net Carbs: 25.5 g
14	Raspberry Walnut Smoothie Bowl with ½ Cup Avocado	Ham and Turkey Club Salad	Enchilada Chicken Bake	Deviled Eggs with Bacon & Creamy Avocado Smoothie	Calories: 1,995 Fat: 157.5 g Protein: 103.5 g Net Carbs: 30 g

Week 3 Meal Plan

Day	Breakfast	Lunch	Dinner	Snack/Dessert	Calories/Macros
15	Chorizo Egg Skillet with ½ Medium Avocado	Hearty Hamburger Salad	Parmesan Crusted Halibut	Toasted Pumpkin Seeds & Chocolate Protein Smoothie	Calories: 1,950 Fat: 157 g Protein: 106 g Net Carbs: 24 g
16	Chocolate Chip Waffles	Fried White Fish Cakes with ½ Medium Avocado	Beef and Mushroom Stroganoff	Leftover Toasted Pumpkin Seeds & Almond Butter Cookies	Calories: 1,980 Fat: 150.5 g Protein: 114.5 g Net Carbs: 29.5 g
17	Leftover Chorizo Egg Skillet with ½ Cup Avocado	Leftover Fried White Fish Cakes	Leftover Beef and Mushroom Stroganoff	Macadamia Blueberry Squares & Cherry Coconut Smoothie	Calories: 1,990 Fat: 165 g Protein: 92 g Net Carbs: 33 g
18	Peanut Butter Breakfast Smoothie	Beefy Cabbage Stew	Pesto Grilled Pork Chops	Chia Coconut Bites & Leftover Almond Butter Cookies	Calories: 2,000 Fat: 157 g Protein: 113 g Net Carbs: 24 g
19	Cheddar Sausage Egg Muffins with ½ Cup Avocado	Pepperoni Pan Pizza	Bacon-Wrapped Stuffed Meatballs	Leftover Chia Coconut Bites & Power Greens Smoothie	Calories: 1,985 Fat: 156.6 g Protein: 110.5 g Net Carbs: 24.5 g

Week 3 Meal Plan				
Day	Breakfast	Lunch	Dinner	Snack/Dessert	Calories/Macros
20	Leftover Cheddar Sausage Egg Muffins	Quick Roast Beef Casserole with 1 Cup Avocado	Cauliflower Fried Rice with Beef	Cocoa Chocolate Fat Bombs & Leftover Almond Butter Cookies	Calories: 1,915 Fat: 154.5 g Protein: 96.5 g Net Carbs: 27 g
21	Omelet with Bacon and Peppers with ½ Medium Avocado	Leftover Pepperoni Pan Pizza	Leftover Bacon-Wrapped Stuffed Meatballs	Leftover Macadamia Blueberry Squares & Cucumber Avocado Smoothie	Calories: 1,980 Fat: 155.5 g Protein: 103 g Net Carbs: 26.5 g

How to Create Your Own Meal Plan

If you prefer to choose your own recipes, or if you have completed the 21-day meal plan, you can work on creating a meal plan of your own. It's really quite simple.

Start by browsing ketogenic recipe collections for dishes that interest you. Compile a collection of recipes for breakfast, lunch, and dinner as well as side dishes, snacks, and desserts. If the calories are not already calculated for each, find an online recipe calculator and plug in the ingredients then note the calories and macros in a spreadsheet that you can refer to when putting the meal plan together.

Once you have all of your recipes, start doing some mix-and-match math work to find combinations that fit within your daily calorie count and macros. Be sure to take note of the ingredients for each recipe so you can find recipes that have overlapping ingredients and don't forget to make a note of the serving sizes as well. It may take some time at first but eventually you'll get the hang of it and you'll become a whiz at creating custom meal plans.

Tips for Quick Meals and Eating Out

The key to success with any diet is sticking to it. Unfortunately, this is life and sometimes there are hiccups in even our best-laid plans. There may be a day here and there when you simply can't stick to the meal plan. For example, if you are traveling and you don't have time to cook, or if you are going out to dinner with friends.

For the periodic moments when you can't cook one of the meals and you need something quick to tide you over, here are some quick-and-easy ideas:

- Bulletproof coffee (mix 20g butter and 10g MCT oil into 1 cup black coffee)
- Eat a few spoonfuls of nut butter from the jar or spread it on celery
- Stir some coconut oil into your coffee or tea for a morning fat boost
- Blend chia seeds with water or almond milk and a pinch of sweetener
- Nibble on a few squares of dark chocolate or cheese
- Mixing in a couple of avocados and mashed hard-boiled eggs with sea salt to taste

If you're going out to dinner and need some tips for sticking to your diet, here are a few simple suggestions:

- Look up the menu ahead of time and plan what you're going to order
- Avoid pasta and rice dishes as well as breaded and fried foods
- Stick to simple protein-and-veggie meals like steak with steamed veggies
- For salads, opt for simple oil and vinegar instead of sugary dressings
- Go for a burger without the bun and load up on avocado, cheese, and bacon
- For dessert, ask for whipped cream and berries or a cheese plate

The longer you follow the ketogenic diet, the better you will get at identifying keto-friendly foods. It'll take some practice, but you'll get the hang of it!

Phase 4: Troubleshooting and Dealing with the Side Effects

As you get started with the 21-day meal plan provided, you may run into some snags along the way. If you've been testing for ketones and you still aren't seeing the number you want, you might need to take a look at how closely you're following the meal plan and search for hidden carbs and sugars.

Start by asking yourself honestly how closely you are following the meal plan. Are you actually following the recipes and serving suggestions or are you making substitutions and eating more than recommended? If that's not the problem, take a look at the ingredients you're using. Are you relying too heavily on sugary or high-carb condiments like ketchup and salad dressing? If so, you might need to cut back or switch to reduced sugar or low-carb alternatives.

Another place you might look for problems is your protein intake. The 21-day meal plan is designed to keep you within the optimal 75/20/5 macronutrient ratio. If you're going off the meal plan and eating more protein than recommended, that could be what's getting in the way of reaching ketosis.

It could also be that you are not consuming enough fats, so it might be good to pop in and have a look at that. Remember we talked about the staple foods of the keto diet earlier? This is where they come in handy. The usual sources of fat that circle in my mind when it comes to adding or drizzling into food would be extra virgin olive oil as well as the good old butter, grass-fed if you can but never margarine! Margarine is a major source of trans fats and those are really bad for the body.

Coconut oil and MCT oil are great for just plain consumption or mixing into coffee or tea. If the nutty taste of coconut oil is too much for you, swap it out for MCT oil. If the fat count still falls short, you have the liberty to consume as much dark chocolate as needed for the fat quota, but make sure it is more than 90% dark. Anything lesser and you run the risk of getting an overload of carbs due to the sugar and dairy in it. Personally, I always go for the 99% variety.

In addition to addressing problems with your ketogenic diet, you should also be on the lookout for certain side effects. As mentioned earlier, the potential side effects of switching to the ketogenic diet include the following:

- Low energy levels
- Brain fog or confusion
- Increased hunger/cravings
- Problems with sleep
- Nausea or stomach upset
- Bad breath
- Leg cramps or soreness
- Changes in bowel habits
- Electrolyte imbalance
- Headaches or migraines

If you're sticking to the meal plan, you should make it through the transition and into full ketosis within a week or two. At that point, your symptoms should subside, and you'll likely begin feeling better than you ever have. In the meantime, some things you can do to mitigate side effects include slowly tapering off carbs, drinking plenty of water, taking a multivitamin for added micronutrients, and getting plenty of sleep. Let's take a look at each side effect and I'll share how best to deal with them along the way.

Low energy levels come about because of the transition from burning carbs to fats, there is this period when brain fog as well as hunger pangs or cravings might get really prominent because your body has not adjusted to burning fats while it simply cannot find sufficient carbs to power on. The best way to deal with these has always been to rest. Give the body the break it needs and don't stress it more by forcing it to work through the low energy barrier. For folks who do not have the luxury of staying at home while the body adjusts, taking quick power naps during work would help. Drinking more water during this period helps too, it staves off the fatigue and also takes the edge off the hunger pangs. Try munching on cheese or pats of butter if the hunger really gets to you.

Stomach upset as well as changes in bowel habits might also occur during the transition phase, primarily because of carb withdrawal. During this time, getting in some probiotics sparingly might be a good idea while the answer to constipation would be to get the optimal amount of hydration. This is also where the coconut water, taken on a daily basis will help out as well.

Coconut water also helps with righting the electrolyte imbalance as well as smoothing out those pesky muscle cramps. Just remember to resist the urge to get in more than one small cup per day! Mixing in one teaspoon of sea salt or table salt with a glass of water can also alleviate the cramps.

Some may also encounter difficulties with disrupted sleep patterns and migraines. During the transition phase, water weight is usually lost first. That is partially the reason why some may wake up in the middle of the night just to relieve themselves, hence disrupting their sleep. This should not deter anyone from staying well hydrated. For this particular problem, you usually have to see it out, and it does pass within a couple of days. Headaches brought on by the reduction of carbs can be alleviated by taking in some moderate amounts of hot tea.

Rest is also a source of relief, though I know it might be tougher to get rest while juggling the demands of work and family.

Lastly, for bad breath, try brushing after every meal and gargling with mouth wash. This does not solve the root of the problem – in fact, having keto inspired bad breath is a sign that you are well on your way to ketosis, but it does lessen the unpleasant smell and makes it better for the folks around you. Chewing on mint leaves will also help, but ignore the mint flavored sweets or gum. Remember, read the labels even more carefully when any sweet or candy proclaims itself to be sugar free. As long as you see that the carb content is high enough to bust your daily limit, rather do without.

Chapter 6
Ooh So Delicious! Easy High-Fat Keto Recipes

Now that you've reviewed the 21-day meal plan, you're ready to get started! In this section, you'll find a collection of more than 80 keto-friendly recipes to enjoy over the next three weeks. These recipes are easy to prepare and full of flavor, so you'll have no trouble sticking to the diet!

As you get started, you may notice that not all of the recipes included in this book are included in the meal plan. To prevent you from having to prepare four unique recipes every day, the meal plan provided makes use of leftovers. The extra recipes are available if you want to cook more often or if you want to swap out one of the recipes in the meal plan – just make sure that the calories and macros fit into your individual calorie/macro goals.

Breakfast Recipes:

- Biscuits with Gravy (pg 61)
- Mexican-Style Scrambled Eggs (pg 62)
- Bacon-Wrapped Spinach Quiches (pg 63)
- Breakfast Pizza Skillet (pg 64)
- Bacon Zucchini Hash (pg 65)
- Breakfast Pockets (pg 67)
- Chocolate Coconut Pancakes (pg 68)
- Cheddar Sausage Omelet (pg 69)
- Chocolate Mocha Chia Pudding (pg 70)
- Vanilla Protein Smoothie (pg 71)
- Jalapeno Cheddar Waffles (pg 72)
- Lamb and Cheddar Breakfast Casserole (pg 73)
- Raspberry Walnut Smoothie Bowl (pg 74)

- Chorizo Egg Skillet (pg 75)
- Veggie Mozzarella Quiche (pg 77)
- Chocolate Chip Waffles pg 78)
- Spiced Almond Muffins (pg 79)
- Cheddar Sausage Egg Muffins (pg 80)
- Peanut Butter Breakfast Smoothie (pg 81)
- Omelet with Bacon and Peppers (pg 82)
- Single-Serve French Toast (pg 84)

Pork and Poultry Recipes:

- Rosemary Apple Pork Tenderloin (pg 111)
- Enchilada Chicken Bake (pg 112)
- Coconut Chicken Curry (pg 113)
- Pork-Stuffed Zucchini Boats (pg 114)
- Sausage and Cabbage Skillet (pg 116)
- Pesto Grilled Pork Chops (pg 117)
- Pan-Seared Lemon Rosemary Chicken (pg 118)
- Pork Egg Roll Bowl (pg 87)
- Ham and Turkey Club Salad (pg 102)
- BLT Sandwich (pg 86)

Beef and Lamb Recipes:

- Beef and Mushroom Stroganoff (pg 119)
- Grilled Steak Kebabs (pg 120)
- Lamb Chops with Herb Butter (pg 121)
- Cauliflower Fried Rice with Beef (pg 122)
- Bacon-Wrapped Stuffed Meatballs (pg 124)
- Ribeye Steak with Green Beans (pg 125)
- Cauliflower and Steak Skillet (pg 126)
- Broccoli Cheddar Casserole with Lamb (pg 127)
- Beefy Cheddar Tacos (pg 89)
- Spinach and Steak Salad (pg 93)
- Beefy Cabbage Stew (pg 94)
- Hearty Hamburger Salad (pg 97)

- Pepperoni Pan Pizza (pg 98)
- Gyro Salad with Avocado Tzatziki (pg 99)
- Beef and Cheese Taco Skillet (pg 100)
- Quick Roast Beef Casserole (pg 103)
- Beef and Veggie Soup (pg 105)
- Meaty Pizza Casserole (pg 107)
- Cheddar-Stuffed Burgers (pg 108)

Seafood Recipes:

- Creamy Fish Chowder (pg 88)
- Fried White Fish Cakes (pg 109)
- Shrimp Zoodle Alfredo (pg 129)
- Seared Salmon with Sautéed Kale (pg 130)
- Dijon-Baked Salmon (pg 133)
- Broccoli White Fish Casserole (pg 134)
- Parmesan Crusted Halibut (pg 131)
- Shrimp Scampi with Spaghetti Squash (pg 135)

Vegetarian Recipes:

- Creamy Cauliflower Soup (pg 91)
- Warm Zucchini Walnut Salad (pg 92)
- Spinach Goat Cheese Pie (pg 95)
- Easy Egg Salad (pg 104)
- Apple Walnut Salad (pg 106)

Snack Recipes:

- Guacamole Deviled Eggs (pg 137)
- Curry Spiced Almonds (pg 138)
- Chia Peanut Butter Bites (pg 139)
- Cheesy Sausage Dip (pg 140)
- Salted Kale Chips (pg 141)
- Bacon Jalapeno Quick Bread (pg 142)
- Toasted Pumpkin Seeds (pg 143)
- Bacon-Wrapped Burger Bites (pg 144)

Desserts and Drinks:

- Power Greens Smoothie (pg 178)
- Cucumber Avocado Smoothie (pg 179)

As an added bonus, I have actually prepared recipe cards for more than two dozen selected recipes. They come with high definition color images of the dishes in a fully printable pdf that you can print out easily for quick reference! Best part is, they are yours! For free!

Just go to the link below and get yours!

www.fcmediapublishing.com/recipecardsrw1

That is recipecards with a rw and finally a digit 1.

Follow the simple one step instruction and you will have the recipe cards emailed to you!

Breakfast Recipes

Biscuits with Gravy

Servings: 2

Serving Size: about ½ recipe

Prep Time: 15 minutes

Cook Time: 25 minutes

Ingredients:

- ¼ cup almond flour
- ½ teaspoon baking powder
- ¼ teaspoon salt
- 1 large egg white
- 6 ounces breakfast sausage, crumbled
- ¼ cup chicken broth
- ¼ cup cream cheese
- Salt and pepper to taste

Instructions:

1. Preheat the oven to 400°F and line a baking sheet with parchment.
2. In a mixing bowl, whisk together the almond flour, baking powder, and salt.
3. In a separate bowl, beat the egg white to stiff peaks.
4. Cut the butter into the dry ingredients to form a crumbled mixture.
5. Fold the crumbled mixture into the egg whites to form a batter.
6. Split the batter into 2 drops for 2 biscuits on the parchment-lined baking sheet.

7. Bake for 11 to 15 minutes until the biscuits are browned then remove to cool.
8. Heat the sausage in a skillet over medium-high heat.
9. Cook the sausage until browned then stir in chicken broth and cream cheese.
10. Simmer until thickened then season with salt and pepper.
11. Serve the biscuits warm with gravy spooned over top.

Nutrition: 425 calories, 36g fat, 22g protein, 2g net carbs

Breakfast Recipes

Mexican-Style Scrambled Eggs

Servings: 1

Serving Size: 1 recipe

Prep Time: 5 minutes

Cook Time: 10 minutes

Ingredients:

- 2 teaspoons coconut oil
- 1 small tomato, diced
- 1 scallion, sliced thin
- 1 tablespoon minced jalapeno
- 1 clove garlic, minced
- 3 large eggs
- 1 tablespoon heavy cream
- 1 ounce shredded Mexican cheese
- Salt and pepper to taste

Instructions:

1. Heat the oil in a skillet over medium heat then add the tomato, scallion, jalapeno, and garlic.
2. Sauté for 3 minutes or until the vegetables are tender.
3. Whisk together the eggs, heavy cream, cheese, salt, and pepper in a bowl.
4. Pour the mixture into the skillet and scramble the eggs to your preference.

Nutrition: 470 calories, 39g fat, 26.5g protein, 6g net carbs

---

Breakfast Recipes

Bacon-Wrapped Spinach Quiches

Servings: 3

Serving Size: 1 quiche

Prep Time: 15 minutes

Cook Time: 20 minutes

Ingredients:

- 3 slices bacon
- 1 tablespoon butter
- 1 medium yellow onion, diced
- 2 cups fresh baby spinach
- 5 large eggs
- 2 ounces shredded cheddar cheese
- Salt and pepper to taste

Instructions:

1. Preheat the oven to 350°F and grease three 4-inch ramekins.
2. Cover the sides and bottoms of each ramekin with slices of bacon.
3. Heat the butter in a skillet over medium-high heat and sauté the onion until brown.
4. Stir in the spinach and cook for 1 to 2 minutes until wilted then divide among the three ramekins.
5. Beat the eggs with the salt and pepper then pour into the ramekins.
6. Bake for 20 minutes until the tops are browned.

Nutrition: 300 calories, 22.5g fat, 20g protein, 4g net carbs

---

Breakfast Recipes

Breakfast Pizza Skillet

Servings: 4

Serving Size: about ¼ recipe

Prep Time: 15 minutes

Cook Time: 25 minutes

Ingredients:

- 6 ounces ground sausage
- 1 medium red pepper, chopped
- 1 medium yellow onion, chopped

- 6 large eggs
- ¼ cup heavy cream
- Salt and pepper to taste

Instructions:

1. Preheat the oven to 350°F.
2. Heat the sausage in a cast-iron skillet until browned, about 5 to 6 minutes.
3. Add the peppers and onions and cook for 4 minutes, or until tender.
4. Remove the mixture to a bowl and reheat the skillet.
5. Beat together the eggs, heavy cream, salt, and pepper then pour into the skillet.
6. Cook for 3 to 4 minutes until the eggs start to set on the bottom.
7. Transfer the skillet to the oven and bake for 20 minutes or until the egg is browned.
8. Spoon the sausage and veggies over top and sprinkle with cheese.
9. Place under the broiler for 3 to 4 minutes until the cheese is melted and browned.
10. Cool the pizza for 5 minutes, then slice and serve.

Nutrition: 595 calories, 45g fat, 37g protein, 9g net carbs

Breakfast Recipes

Bacon Zucchini Hash

Servings: 1

Serving Size: 1 recipe

Prep Time: 10 minutes

Cook Time: 20 minutes

Ingredients:

- 1 tablespoon coconut oil
- 1 small yellow onion, chopped
- 1 clove garlic, minced
- 2 slices bacon, chopped
- 1 small zucchini, diced
- 2 large eggs
- Salt and pepper to taste

Instructions:

1. Heat the oil in a skillet over medium heat and add the onion and garlic.
2. Cook for 3 minutes, stirring often, then stir in the chopped bacon.
3. Let it cook until the bacon is crispy then stir in the zucchini.
4. Sauté the mixture for 12 minutes then push it to the sides of the skillet.
5. Crack the eggs into the center and season with salt and pepper.
6. Cook the eggs to your preference and serve over the hash.

Nutrition: 415 calories, 32g fat, 22g protein 9.5g net carbs

Breakfast Recipes

Breakfast Pockets

Servings: 2

Serving Size: ½ pocket

Prep Time: 15 minutes

Cook Time: 25 minutes

Ingredients:

- 3 ounces shredded mozzarella cheese
- 1 tablespoon butter
- 3 large eggs, whisked
- 4 slices bacon, chopped
- 1 ounce shredded cheddar cheese
- ¼ cup almond flour

Instructions:

1. Preheat the oven to 400°F and line a baking sheet with parchment.
2. In a microwave-safe bowl, melt the mozzarella in the microwave then stir in the almond flour.
3. Place the dough on a sheet of parchment paper, top with another piece and roll out flat.
4. Heat the butter in a skillet over medium-high heat.
5. Add the eggs and scramble until cooked to your preference then spread over the dough.
6. Top with chopped bacon and shredded cheddar cheese.
7. Fold the dough over and seal the edges then cut a few slits to vent steam.

8. Bake for 20 minutes until golden brown. Cool slightly before serving.

Nutrition: 440 calories, 33.5g fat, 32g protein, 2.5g net carbs

---

Breakfast Recipes

Chocolate Coconut Pancakes

Servings: 1

Serving Size: 1 recipe

Prep Time: 10 minutes

Cook Time: 10 minutes

Ingredients:

- 2 large eggs, whisked
- 1 tablespoon butter, melted
- 2 tablespoons coconut flour
- 1 scoop chocolate whey protein powder
- ¼ teaspoon baking soda
- Pinch salt
- 1 tablespoon coconut oil

Instructions:

1. Heat a cast-iron skillet over medium heat.
2. Beat together the eggs and melted butter in a mixing bowl.
3. Whisk in the coconut flour, protein powder, baking soda, and salt.

4. Melt the coconut oil in the skillet then spoon the batter into three circles.
5. Cook until bubbles form on the surface of the batter.
6. Flip the pancakes and cook until browned on both sides. Serve with powdered erythritol.

Nutrition: 535 calories, 40g fat, 27g protein, 8.5g net carbs

---

Breakfast Recipes

<u>Cheddar Sausage Omelet</u>

Servings: 1

Serving Size: 1 omelet

Prep Time: 5 minutes

Cook Time: 15 minutes

Ingredients:

- 2 large eggs
- 1 tablespoon heavy cream
- Pinch each of salt and pepper
- 3 ounces ground pork sausage
- 2 tablespoons diced yellow onion
- ¼ cup shredded cheddar cheese

Instructions:

1. Whisk together the eggs, heavy cream, salt and pepper.
2. Cook the sausage in a skillet over medium-high heat then stir in the onions.

3. Sauté the mixture until the onions are translucent, about 3 to 4 minutes.
4. Remove the mixture to a bowl and reheat the skillet.
5. Add the butter and let it melt then pour in the egg mixture.
6. Cook for 2 minutes until the bottom of the egg is almost set.
7. Spoon the sausage mixture over half the egg and sprinkle with cheese.
8. Fold the omelet over and cook until just set. Serve hot.

Nutrition: 545 calories, 43g fat, 33g protein, 5g net carbs

Breakfast Recipes

Chocolate Mocha Chia Pudding

Servings: 2

Serving Size: ½ recipe

Prep Time: 5 minutes

Cook Time: 0 minutes

Ingredients:

- 1 cup brewed coffee
- ⅓ cup canned coconut milk
- 1 scoop chocolate whey protein powder
- 1 tablespoon vanilla extract
- 1 tablespoon powdered erythritol
- ⅓ cup chia seeds
- 1 tablespoon unsweetened cocoa powder

Instructions:

1. Brew a cup of coffee and pour it into a mixing bowl to cool.
2. Add the coconut milk, protein powder, vanilla, and powdered erythritol.
3. Whisk in the chia seeds and cocoa powder then spoon into two glass jars.
4. Cover the jars and chill for at least 30 minutes until thickened.

Nutrition: 320 calories, 25g fat, 15.5g protein, 6.5g net carbs

---

Breakfast Recipes

Vanilla Protein Smoothie

Servings: 1

Serving Size: 1 recipe

Prep Time: 5 minutes

Cook Time: 0 minutes

Ingredients:

- ½ cup heavy cream
- ¼ cup unsweetened almond milk
- 1 scoop vanilla whey protein powder
- 1 tablespoon coconut oil
- 1 tablespoon powdered erythritol
- ½ teaspoon vanilla extract
- 4 to 5 ice cubes

- 2 tablespoons whipped cream

Instructions:

1. Combine the heavy cream, almond milk, protein powder, coconut oil, and powdered erythritol in a blender.
2. Add the vanilla and ice cubes, then blend until smooth.
3. Pour into a glass and top with whipped cream to serve.

Nutrition: 500 calories, 43g fat, 24g protein, 4.5g net carbs

---

Breakfast Recipes

Jalapeno Cheddar Waffles

Servings: 3

Serving Size: 1 waffle

Prep Time: 10 minutes

Cook Time: 15 minutes

Ingredients:

- 1 medium head cauliflower, cooked and chopped
- 8 ounces ham, diced
- 4 green onions, sliced thin
- ¼ cup shredded cheddar cheese
- 2 large eggs
- 1 jalapeno, seeded and minced
- Sour cream, to serve

Instructions:

1. Put the cauliflower in a food processor and pulse into grains that resemble rice.
2. Transfer the cauliflower to a bowl and stir in the diced ham, sliced green onions, cheddar cheese, eggs, and jalapeno.
3. Heat a waffle iron to high heat then spoon ½ cup of batter into it.
4. Close the waffle iron and cook until the waffle is golden brown then remove.
5. Repeat with the remaining batter and serve with sour cream.

Nutrition: 265 calories, 13g fat, 23g protein, 9.5g net carbs

---

Breakfast Recipes

Lamb and Cheddar Breakfast Casserole

Servings: 3

Serving Size: about ⅓ recipe

Prep Time: 15 minutes

Cook Time: 35 minutes

Ingredients:

- 6 ounces ground lamb
- 4 slices bacon, chopped
- 1 medium yellow onion, chopped
- 1 clove garlic, minced
- 5 large eggs

- 2 tablespoons heavy cream
- Salt and pepper to taste
- 2 ounces shredded cheddar cheese
- 2 green onions, sliced thin

Instructions:

1. Preheat the oven to 350°F and lightly grease a small casserole dish.
2. Combine the lamb and bacon in a skillet over medium-high heat and cook until the lamb is browned, breaking it into pieces.
3. Stir in the onions and garlic then cook for 3 minutes until browned.
4. Spread the mixture evenly in the casserole dish.
5. Whisk together the eggs, heavy cream, salt and pepper then pour into the dish.
6. Sprinkle with cheese and bake for 30 to 35 minutes until set.
7. Top with sliced green onions and serve hot.

Nutrition: 425 calories, 28g fat, 37g protein, 4.5g net carbs

---

Breakfast Recipes

Raspberry Walnut Smoothie Bowl

Servings: 1

Serving Size: 1 recipe

Prep Time: 10 minutes

Cook Time: 0 minutes

Ingredients:

- 1 cup fresh baby spinach
- ½ cup unsweetened almond milk
- 2 tablespoons heavy cream
- 1 tablespoon coconut oil
- 1 scoop whey protein powder
- 5 fresh raspberries
- 1 tablespoon toasted walnuts, chopped
- 1 tablespoon flaked coconut

Instructions:

1. Place the spinach and almond milk in a blender and blend until smooth.
2. Add the heavy cream, coconut oil, and protein powder then blend again.
3. Throw in a few ice cubes and blend to thicken, if desired.
4. Pour the smoothie into a bowl and top with raspberries, walnuts, and coconut.

Nutrition: 485 calories, 35g fat, 27g protein, 11g net carbs

Breakfast Recipes

Chorizo Egg Skillet

Servings: 4

Serving Size: about ¼ recipe

Prep Time: 10 minutes

Cook Time: 30 minutes

Ingredients:

- 1 tablespoon coconut oil
- 12 ounces ground chorizo sausage
- 1 medium red pepper, chopped
- 1 medium yellow onion, chopped
- 2 cloves garlic, minced
- ½ tablespoon chili powder
- 1 ½ teaspoons ground cumin
- Salt and pepper to taste
- 1 (14-ounce) can diced tomatoes
- 4 large eggs
- 2 ounces queso fresco, crumbled

Instructions:

1. Heat the coconut oil in a large skillet over medium heat and add the chorizo.
2. Cook the chorizo until browned, breaking it up into pieces.
3. Remove the chorizo into a bowl and reheat the skillet to medium-high heat.
4. Add the peppers and onions and cook for 5 minutes.
5. Stir in the garlic, chili powder, and cumin then season with salt and pepper.
6. Add the chorizo back into the skillet along with the tomatoes – simmer for 5 minutes.
7. Spread the mixture evenly in the skillet and make 6 depressions.
8. Crack an egg into each depression and season with salt and pepper.
9. Cook until the eggs are done to your liking and serve with queso fresco.

Nutrition: 450 calories, 37g fat, 23.5g protein, 11g net carbs

Breakfast Recipes

<u>Veggie Mozzarella Quiche</u>

Servings: 4

Serving Size: about ¼ recipe

Prep Time: 15 minutes

Cook Time: 25 minutes

Ingredients:

- 2 cups shredded mozzarella cheese
- 1 tablespoon butter
- 1 medium yellow onion, chopped
- 1 medium red pepper, chopped
- 1 cup diced cauliflower
- 6 large eggs, whisked
- 1 cup heavy cream
- 1 teaspoon dried thyme
- Salt and pepper to taste

Instructions:

1. Preheat the oven to 350°F and lightly grease a 10-inch quiche pan.
2. Add the mozzarella cheese to the pan and spread it evenly then set aside.
3. Heat the butter in a skillet over medium heat.
4. Add the onion, peppers, and cauliflower and cook until tender, about 5 minutes.
5. Spoon the veggie mixture into the quiche pan and spread evenly.

6. Beat the eggs with the heavy cream, thyme, salt, and pepper.
7. Pour the mixture into the quiche pan and bake for 20 to 25 minutes until set.
8. Let the quiche cool for 5 to 10 minutes before slicing to serve.

Nutrition: 305 calories, 24g fat, 15g protein, 6.5g net carbs

---

Breakfast Recipes

Chocolate Chip Waffles

Servings: 2

Serving Size: 1 waffle

Prep Time: 10 minutes

Cook Time: 15 minutes

Ingredients:

- 2 large eggs, yolks and whites separated
- 3 scoops whey protein powder
- 2 tablespoons butter, melted
- ½ teaspoon vanilla extract
- 50g cocoa nibs

Instructions:

1. Beat the egg whites to stiff peaks then set aside.
2. In a mixing bowl, whisk the protein powder with the melted butter, egg yolks, and vanilla extract.

3. Fold in the beaten egg whites and cocoa nibs until well combined.
4. Grease and preheat a waffle iron to high heat.
5. Spoon half the batter into the waffle iron then close and cook until browned.
6. Repeat with the remaining batter and serve warm with butter.

Nutrition: 505 calories, 31g fat, 40g protein, 11g net carbs

Breakfast Recipes

Spiced Almond Muffins

Servings: 3

Serving Size: 2 muffins

Prep Time: 10 minutes

Cook Time: 25 minutes

Ingredients:

- 1 cup almond flour
- ½ cup powdered erythritol
- 1 teaspoon baking powder
- 1 teaspoon ground cinnamon
- ¼ teaspoon ground nutmeg
- Pinch salt
- ⅓ cup almond butter
- ½ cup unsweetened almond milk
- 2 large eggs, whisked
- 1 ounce thinly sliced almonds

Instructions:

1. Preheat the oven to 350°F and line half of a muffin tray (six of the cups) with paper liners.
2. Combine the almond flour, powdered erythritol, baking powder, cinnamon, nutmeg, and salt in a mixing bowl.
3. In a microwave-safe bowl, melt the almond butter then stir it into the almond milk.
4. Stir the almond milk mixture into the dry ingredients then beat in the eggs.
5. Spoon the mixture evenly into each cup in the muffin pan and top with sliced almonds.
6. Bake for 20 to 25 minutes until a knife inserted in the center comes out clean.

Nutrition: 295 calories, 24.5g fat, 12.5g protein, 6g net carbs

---

Breakfast Recipes

Cheddar Sausage Egg Muffins

Servings: 4

Serving Size: 3 muffins

Prep Time: 10 minutes

Cook Time: 30 minutes

Ingredients:

- 12 ounces breakfast sausage
- 1 medium yellow onion, chopped

- 1 small red pepper, chopped
- 1 clove garlic, minced
- Salt and pepper to taste
- 3 large eggs
- 2 tablespoons heavy cream
- ½ cup shredded cheddar cheese

Instructions:

1. Preheat the oven to 350°F and grease a muffin pan with cooking spray.
2. Combine the sausage, onion, red pepper, garlic, salt and pepper in a bowl.
3. Stir well then divide the mixture evenly in the pan, pressing it into the cups.
4. Beat the eggs with the heavy cream then pour into the cups and top with cheese.
5. Bake for 25 to 30 minutes until the eggs are set and the cheese browned.

Nutrition: 445 calories, 35.5g fat, 25.5g protein, 5g net carbs

---

Breakfast Recipes

Peanut Butter Breakfast Smoothie

Servings: 1

Serving Size: 1 recipe

Prep Time: 5 minutes

Cook Time: 0 minutes

Ingredients:

- 1 ¼ cup unsweetened almond milk
- ¼ cup canned coconut milk
- 2 tablespoons peanut butter
- 1 scoop whey protein powder
- 5 to 6 drops liquid stevia extract
- ½ teaspoon vanilla extract
- 4 to 5 ice cubes

Instructions:

1. Combine the almond milk, coconut milk, peanut butter, protein powder, and liquid stevia extract in a blender.
2. Add the vanilla and ice cubes then blend until smooth.
3. Pour into a glass and top with whipped cream to serve.

Nutrition: 500 calories, 36.5g fat, 33g protein, 10.5g net carbs

---

Breakfast Recipes

Omelet with Bacon and Peppers

Servings: 1

Serving Size: 1 omelet

Prep Time: 5 minutes

Cook Time: 15 minutes

Ingredients:

- 2 slices bacon, uncooked
- ¼ cup diced yellow onion
- ¼ cup diced red pepper
- 3 large eggs
- 1 tablespoon heavy cream
- Salt to taste
- 2 tablespoons shredded cheddar cheese

Instructions:

1. Cook the bacon in a skillet until crisp, then remove to paper towels.
2. Reheat the skillet with the bacon grease, then add the onions and peppers.
3. Cook until the veggies are tender, then remove to a bowl.
4. Beat the eggs with the heavy cream and salt, then pour into the skillet
5. Cook until the egg starts to set, then spoon the veggies over half.
6. Chop the bacon and sprinkle over the veggies, then add the cheese.
7. Cook until the egg is set and serve hot.

Nutrition: 425 calories, 29.5g fat, 30g protein, 6g net carbs

Breakfast Recipes

Single-Serve French Toast

Servings: 1

Serving Size: 1 recipe

Prep Time: 5 minutes

Cook Time: 10 minutes

Ingredients:

- 1 tablespoon butter
- 2 large eggs
- 1 tablespoon coconut flour
- 1 ½ teaspoons cream cheese
- ½ teaspoon baking powder
- ¼ teaspoon ground cinnamon
- Pinch ground nutmeg
- ¼ cup heavy cream
- 1 teaspoon coconut oil

Instructions:

1. Melt the butter in a 6-inch ramekin in the microwave.
2. Whisk in one egg along with the coconut flour, cream cheese, baking powder, cinnamon, and nutmeg.
3. Cook on high heat for 90 seconds then cool for one minute.
4. Pop the bread out of the ramekin and wait until it is cool enough to handle then slice in half.
5. Beat the remaining egg with the heavy cream and soak the bread in it.

6. Heat the coconut oil in a skillet over medium-high heat.
7. Add the bread slices and cook until browned on both sides.

Nutrition: 465 calories, 40g fat, 15.5g protein, 6.5g net carbs

Lunch Recipes

BLT Sandwich

Servings: 4

Serving Size: 2 sandwiches

Prep Time: 10 minutes

Cook Time: 25 minutes

Ingredients:

- 3 large eggs, separated
- ¼ cup cream cheese, softened
- ½ tablespoon psyllium husk powder
- ½ teaspoon baking powder
- 4 slices bacon, uncooked
- 4 tablespoons mayonnaise
- 4 leaves romaine lettuce
- 4 slices tomato

Instructions:

1. Preheat the oven to 300°F and line a baking sheet with parchment paper.
2. Beat the egg whites to stiff peaks in a mixing bowl.
3. In a separate bowl, combine the egg yolks with the cream cheese, psyllium, and baking powder.
4. Fold in the egg whites then spoon onto the baking sheet in 8 even circles.
5. Bake for 25 minutes until the edges are browned while you cook the bacon.
6. When the bread circles are cooled, top 4 of them with a tablespoon of mayonnaise.

7. Add lettuce, tomato, and bacon then top with another bread circle to serve.

Nutrition: 440 calories, 35.5g fat, 19g protein, 10.5g net carbs

---

Lunch Recipes

Pork Egg Roll Bowl

Servings: 2

Serving Size: about ½ recipe

Prep Time: 10 minutes

Cook Time: 25 minutes

Ingredients:

- 1 tablespoon olive oil
- 10 ounces ground pork
- 2 cups coleslaw mix (no dressing)
- ½ tablespoon soy sauce
- 1 teaspoon grated ginger
- ½ teaspoon minced garlic
- ½ cup diced avocado
- 4 green onions, sliced thin

Instructions:

1. Heat the oil in a skillet over medium heat then add the pork.
2. Cook until the pork is browned, breaking it into pieces with a spoon.

3. Stir in the coleslaw mix, soy sauce, ginger, and garlic – cook for 3 minutes.
4. Spoon the mixture into two bowls and top with avocado and green onion.

Nutrition: 460 calories, 34.5g fat, 28g protein, 6g net carbs

---

Lunch Recipes

Creamy Fish Chowder

Servings: 6

Serving Size: about 1 ½ cups

Prep Time: 20 minutes

Cook Time: 45 minutes

Ingredients:

- 4 slices bacon, chopped
- 1 medium yellow onion, chopped
- ¼ cup butter
- 1 tablespoon minced garlic
- ¼ cup dry white wine
- 3 cups chicken broth
- 1 medium head cauliflower, chopped
- 1 teaspoon dried thyme
- 2 cups heavy cream
- 1 pound white fish, steamed and flaked

Instructions:

1. Cook the bacon in a large stockpot over low heat for 10 minutes.
2. Stir in the onion and butter, then increase the heat to medium-high.
3. Cook for 5 minutes then stir in the garlic and cook for another 3 minutes.
4. Pour in the wine and deglaze the pan, stirring for 1 minutes while scraping up the browned bits.
5. Stir in the chicken broth, cauliflower, and thyme then bring to a boil.
6. Reduce heat and simmer for 25 minutes then stir in the cream.
7. Simmer for 10 minutes then puree the soup using an immersion blender.
8. Return the pot to low heat and stir in the fish.
9. Adjust the seasoning to taste and serve hot.

Nutrition: 360 calories, 26.5g fat, 21g protein, 6g net carbs

---

Lunch Recipes

<u>Beefy Cheddar Tacos</u>

Servings: 2

Serving Size: about ½ recipe

Prep Time: 15 minutes

Cook Time: 15 minutes

Ingredients:

- 1 ½ cups shredded cheddar cheese
- 5 ounces ground beef (80% lean)
- ½ cup diced tomatoes
- 1 tablespoon taco seasoning
- Salt and pepper to taste
- ¼ cup chopped avocado
- ¼ cup sour cream

Instructions:

1. Preheat the oven to 350°F and line a baking sheet with parchment paper.
2. Spread the cheese in two even-sized circles on the baking sheet.
3. Bake for 6 to 7 minutes until melted and browned around the edges.
4. Let cool for 3 to 4 minutes then drape over a wooden spoon to form a taco shape.
5. Cool the shell until it is completely hard while you prepare the filling.
6. Brown the beef in a skillet then drain the fat.
7. Stir in the tomatoes and taco seasoning then season with salt and pepper.
8. Spoon the filling into the shells and top with sour cream and avocado.

Nutrition: 660 calories, 52g fat, 35g protein, 10g net carbs

Lunch Recipes

Creamy Cauliflower Soup

Servings: 2

Serving Size: about ½ recipe

Prep Time: 10 minutes

Cook Time: 20 minutes

Ingredients:

- 1 teaspoon olive oil
- 1 medium head cauliflower, chopped
- 2 cloves garlic, minced
- 2 cups chicken broth
- 2 ounces cream cheese
- 1 tablespoon butter
- Salt and pepper to taste

Instructions:

1. Heat the oil in a skillet over medium heat.
2. Finely chop a few cauliflower florets and fry in the oil with garlic until browned.
3. Add the rest of the cauliflower to a saucepan with the chicken broth.
4. Bring to a boil then reduce heat and simmer until the cauliflower is tender.
5. Stir in the cream cheese, butter, salt and pepper then puree until smooth.
6. Spoon into bowls and garnish with cauliflower bits.

Nutrition: 285 calories, 20g fat, 13g protein, 10.5g net carbs

Lunch Recipes

Warm Zucchini Walnut Salad

Servings: 1

Serving Size: 1 recipe

Prep Time: 15 minutes

Cook Time: 5 minutes

Ingredients:

- 2 tablespoons coconut milk
- ½ tablespoon olive oil
- 1 clove garlic, minced
- ½ small zucchini (halved lengthwise)
- 1 tablespoon coconut oil
- 1 cup chopped romaine lettuce
- 1 cup chopped spinach
- 1 green onion, sliced thin
- 1 ounce toasted walnuts

Instructions:

1. For the dressing, whisk together the coconut milk, olive oil, and garlic in a small bowl.
2. Scoop the seeds out of the zucchini half and discard, then slice thin.
3. Heat the oil in a skillet over medium-high heat and add the zucchini.
4. Sauté the zucchini until tender then remove from heat.
5. Combine the romaine, spinach, and green onions in a salad bowl and toss with the dressing.

6. Top the salad with the zucchini and walnuts.

Nutrition: 450 calories, 45g fat, 9.5g protein, 4.5g net carbs

---

Lunch Recipes

Spinach and Steak Salad

Servings: 1

Serving Size: 1 recipe

Prep Time: 10 minutes

Cook Time: 10 minutes

Ingredients:

- 1 ½ cups fresh baby spinach
- 1 small tomato, diced
- ¼ cup diced cucumber
- 1 tablespoon butter
- 4 ounces sirloin steak
- Salt and pepper to taste
- ¼ cup diced avocado
- 2 tablespoons fresh lime juice
- 2 tablespoons fresh cilantro
- 1 teaspoon olive oil

Instructions:

1. Toss together the spinach, tomatoes, and cucumber in a salad bowl.
2. Heat the butter over medium-high heat in a skillet.
3. Add the steak and season with salt and pepper.

4. Cook until seared underneath, about 3 to 4 minutes, then flip and cook to your preference.
5. Remove the steak to a cutting board to rest 5 minutes, then slice.
6. Combine the remaining ingredients in a blender and blend smooth.
7. Top the salad with the sliced steak and drizzle with dressing.

Nutrition: 460 calories, 31g fat, 37.5g protein, 5g net carbs

---

Lunch Recipes

<u>Beefy Cabbage Stew</u>

Servings: 4

Serving Size: about ¼ recipe

Prep Time: 10 minutes

Cook Time: 7 hours

Ingredients:

- 4 ounces bacon, chopped
- 1 large red onion, diced
- 1 tablespoon minced garlic
- 1 pound beef chuck roast, boneless
- Salt and pepper to taste
- 1 small head cabbage, sliced thin
- 1 teaspoon fresh chopped thyme
- ½ teaspoon fresh chopped oregano
- ½ cup beef broth

- ½ teaspoon xanthan gum

Instructions:

1. Spread the bacon, onion, and garlic in a slow cooker.
2. Place the chuck roast on top and season with salt and pepper.
3. Add the shredded cabbage and herbs then pour in the broth.
4. Cover and cook on low heat for 6 to 7 hours until the meat is very tender.
5. Remove the roast to a cutting board and stir the xanthan gum into the cooking liquid.
6. Cook on high heat for 15 minutes or until thickened.
7. Shred the beef and serve with the cabbage and thickened sauce.

Nutrition: 635 calories, 44g fat, 43.5g protein, 10g net carbs

---

Lunch Recipes

Spinach Goat Cheese Pie

Servings: 4

Serving Size: about ¼ recipe

Prep Time: 15 minutes

Cook Time: 1 hour

Ingredients:

- 1 cup almond flour
- 2 tablespoons ground flaxseed

- 1 tablespoon psyllium husk powder
- Pinch salt and pepper
- 4 eggs, divided
- ¾ cup heavy cream
- 2 ounces shredded mozzarella cheese
- 1 tablespoon olive oil
- 1 small yellow onion, chopped
- 2 cloves garlic, minced
- 2 cups fresh chopped spinach
- 3 ounces goat cheese

Instructions:

1. Preheat the oven to 350°F and grease a springform pan with oil.
2. Combine the almond flour with the flaxseed, psyllium husk, and a pinch of salt with one egg in a food processor.
3. Pulse the mixture into a dough then press it into the bottom and up the sides of the springform pan.
4. Prick the dough with a fork in several places, then bake for 12 to 15 minutes and let cool.
5. Beat together the other 3 eggs with the heavy cream, mozzarella, salt and pepper.
6. Heat the oil in a large skillet over medium heat and add the onion and garlic.
7. Cook for 3 to 4 minutes, then stir in the spinach and cook for another 2 minutes.
8. Spread the spinach mixture into the springform pan and pour in the eggs.
9. Sprinkle on the goat cheese and bake for 35 to 40 minutes until set.

Nutrition: 445 calories, 35.5g fat, 21.5g protein, 6g net carbs

---

Lunch Recipes

Hearty Hamburger Salad

Servings: 1

Serving Size: 1 recipe

Prep Time: 5 minutes

Cook Time: 15 minutes

Ingredients:

- 5 ounces ground beef (80% lean)
- ¼ teaspoon paprika
- ¼ teaspoon garlic powder
- Salt and pepper to taste
- 1 ½ cups chopped romaine lettuce
- 4 cherry tomatoes, quartered
- ¼ cup diced avocado
- 2 tablespoons shredded cheddar cheese

Instructions:

1. Cook the beef in a skillet over medium-high heat until browned.
2. Drain some of the fat then stir in the spices and season with salt and pepper.
3. In a bowl, toss together the lettuce and tomatoes.
4. Top the salad with the cooked beef, shredded cheese, and avocado.

Nutrition: 480 calories, 37g fat, 29g protein, 3.5g net carbs

---

Lunch Recipes

Pepperoni Pan Pizza

Servings: 3

Serving Size: 1 pizza

Prep Time: 10 minutes

Cook Time: 25 minutes

Ingredients:

- 6 large eggs
- ⅓ cup grated parmesan cheese
- 3 tablespoons psyllium husk powder
- 2 teaspoon dried Italian seasoning
- Pinch salt
- 2 tablespoons coconut oil
- ⅔ cup low-carb tomato sauce (recommended Rao's homemade marinara sauce)
- 2 ounces diced pepperoni
- 1 ½ cups shredded mozzarella cheese

Instructions:

1. Combine the eggs, parmesan, and psyllium husk in a blender.
2. Add the Italian seasoning with a pinch of salt then blend until smooth.
3. Let the batter rest for 5 minutes while you heat the oil in a skillet.

4. Spoon about ⅓ of the batter into the skillet and spread it evenly into a circle.
5. Cook until the crust is browned underneath then flip and brown on the other side.
6. Remove the crust and keep warm then repeat with the remaining batter.
7. Place the three finished crusts on a baking sheet lined with foil.
8. Top with tomato sauce, pepperoni, and cheese then broil until browned.

Nutrition: 450 calories, 35g fat, 25g protein, 3.5g net carbs

---

Lunch Recipes

Gyro Salad with Avocado Tzatziki

Servings: 3

Serving Size: about ⅓ recipe

Prep Time: 10 minutes

Cook Time: 25 minutes

Ingredients:

- 1 tablespoon olive oil
- 1 pound lamb shoulder, sliced
- Salt and pepper to taste
- 1 small yellow onion, chopped
- ¼ cup chicken broth
- 1 tablespoon lemon juice
- ½ teaspoon dried thyme

- ½ teaspoon dried oregano
- ½ medium English cucumber
- 1 medium avocado, pitted and chopped
- 1 tablespoon fresh chopped mint
- 1 teaspoon fresh chopped dill
- 5 cups fresh chopped romaine lettuce

Instructions:

1. Heat the oil in a large skillet over medium high heat.
2. Season the lamb with salt and pepper then add to the skillet.
3. Cook for 2 to 3 minutes then add the onion.
4. Let the mixture cook until the onion is translucent then stir in the chicken broth, lemon juice, oregano and thyme.
5. Simmer for another 5 minutes.
6. Grate the cucumber and wring out as much moisture as possible.
7. Add the cucumber to a food processor with the avocado, mint, and dill, then blend until smooth.
8. Divide the romaine among three salad bowls and top each with lamb and tzatziki.

Nutrition: 485 calories, 29g fat, 45g protein, 5.5g net carbs

---

Lunch Recipes

Beef and Cheese Taco Skillet

Servings: 1

Serving Size: 1 recipe

Prep Time: 10 minutes

Cook Time: 25 minutes

Ingredients:

- 4 ounces ground beef (80% lean)
- 1 small yellow onion, diced
- ½ small red pepper, diced
- ¼ cup diced zucchini
- Salt and pepper to taste
- 1 tablespoon taco seasoning
- 2 tablespoons water
- 1 ounce shredded cheddar cheese
- 1 ½ cups chopped romaine lettuce

Instructions:

1. Cook the beef in a skillet over medium-high heat until browned.
2. Drain some of the fat then stir in the onion, peppers, and zucchini.
3. Season with salt and pepper then sauté for 5 minutes or until the veggies are browned.
4. Stir in the taco seasoning and water, then bring to a simmer and cook for 3 minutes.
5. Sprinkle with cheese and cook for 5 minutes until melted.
6. Spoon the taco mixture over chopped lettuce to serve.

Nutrition: 475 calories, 33g fat, 29g protein, 12g net carbs

Lunch Recipes

<u>Ham and Turkey Club Salad</u>

Servings: 2

Serving Size: ½ recipe

Prep Time: 10 minutes

Cook Time: 0 minutes

Ingredients:

- ¼ cup canned coconut milk
- 2 teaspoons olive oil
- 2 teaspoons Dijon mustard
- Salt and pepper to taste
- 3 cups chopped romaine lettuce
- ½ cup diced tomatoes
- 4 ounces smoked turkey, chopped
- 4 ounces deli ham, chopped
- 2 slices bacon, cooked and chopped

Instructions:

1. Whisk together the coconut milk, olive oil, Dijon mustard, salt and pepper.
2. Toss in the lettuce and tomatoes then divide between two salad plates.
3. Top each with chopped turkey, ham, and bacon.

Nutrition: 355 calories, 26g fat, 24.5g protein, 6g net carbs

Lunch Recipes

Quick Roast Beef Casserole

Servings: 1

Serving Size: 1 recipe

Prep Time: 5 minutes

Cook Time: 25 minutes

Ingredients:

- 4 ounces sliced roast beef
- 1 tablespoon sour cream
- 2 tablespoons canned chilis, diced
- 2 ounces shredded pepper jack cheese
- Pinch paprika

Instructions:

1. Line the bottom of a microwave-safe bowl with slices of roast beef.
2. Spoon ½ tablespoon of sour cream over it and top with half the chilis.
3. Sprinkle with 1 ounce cheese then repeat the layers.
4. Microwave until the cheese is melted then sprinkle with paprika and serve.

Nutrition: 405 calories, 26.5g fat, 38.5g protein, 5g net carbs

Lunch Recipes

<u>Easy Egg Salad</u>

Servings: 2

Serving Size: about ½ recipe

Prep Time: 15 minutes

Cook Time: 0 minutes

Ingredients:

- 3 hard-boiled eggs, cooled
- 2 tablespoons diced celery
- 3 tablespoons canned coconut milk
- 1 tablespoon fresh chopped parsley
- 1 teaspoon fresh lemon juice
- Salt and pepper to taste
- 1 ½ cups chopped romaine lettuce

Instructions:

1. Peel the eggs and chop them coarsely into a mixing bowl.
2. Toss in the celery, coconut milk, parsley, lemon juice, salt and pepper.
3. Spoon the egg salad over chopped romaine to serve.

Nutrition: 300 calories, 24g fat, 18g protein, 3g net carbs

Lunch Recipes

<u>Beef and Veggie Soup</u>

Servings: 3

Serving Size: about 1 ½ cups

Prep Time: 45 minutes

Cook Time: 20 minutes

Ingredients:

- 8 ounces sliced mushrooms
- 1 medium yellow onion, chopped
- 1 cup Brussels sprouts, quartered
- 2 tablespoons olive oil
- Salt and pepper to taste
- 12 ounces beef sirloin, chopped
- 1 tablespoon butter
- 2 cups beef broth
- ½ teaspoon dried oregano
- ¼ teaspoon dried thyme

Instructions:

1. Preheat the oven to 350°F.
2. Toss the mushrooms, onions, and Brussels sprouts in olive oil then spread them in a glass baking dish.
3. Season with salt and pepper then roast for 30 minutes.
4. Brown the beef in a saucepan with the butter over medium heat until cooked through.
5. Add the cooked veggies and the remaining ingredients then bring to a boil.

6. Reduce heat and simmer for 20 minutes then serve hot.

Nutrition: 395 calories, 21.5g fat, 41.5g protein, 6.5g net carbs

---

Lunch Recipes

Apple Walnut Salad

Servings: 2

Serving Size: ½ recipe

Prep Time: 10 minutes

Cook Time: 0 minutes

Ingredients:

- 6 tablespoons canned coconut milk
- 1 tablespoon fresh lemon juice
- 1 teaspoon Dijon mustard
- Salt and pepper to taste
- ½ cup diced apple
- ½ cup diced celery
- ¼ cup toasted walnut halves
- 3 cups chopped romaine lettuce

Instructions:

1. Whisk together the coconut milk, lemon juice, Dijon mustard, salt and pepper.
2. In a large salad bowl, combine the apples, celery, and walnuts.

3. Toss the mixture with the dressing to coat then serve over chopped romaine.

Nutrition: 445 calories, 40.5g fat, 11g protein, 12g net carbs

---

Lunch Recipes

Meaty Pizza Casserole

Servings: 3

Serving Size: about ⅓ recipe

Prep Time: 20 minutes

Cook Time: 25 minutes

Ingredients:

- 1 tablespoon olive oil
- 8 ounces ground Italian sausage
- 4 ounces ground beef (80% lean)
- 1 small red pepper, chopped
- 1 medium yellow onion, chopped
- 8 ounces sliced mushrooms
- 1 cup shredded mozzarella cheese
- 2 ounces diced pepperoni

Instructions:

1. Preheat the oven to 400°F and grease a square baking dish with cooking spray.
2. Heat the oil in a skillet over medium-high heat.
3. Add the sausage, beef, peppers, and onions and cook for 6 minutes.

4. Spread the mixture in the baking dish then set aside.
5. Cook the mushrooms in butter until browned then spread in the dish.
6. Sprinkle with cheese and diced pepperoni then bake for 25 minutes.

Nutrition: 500 calories, 35g fat, 35g protein, 8.5g net carbs

---

Lunch Recipes

Cheddar-Stuffed Burgers

Servings: 2

Serving Size: 1 burger

Prep Time: 10 minutes

Cook Time: 15 minutes

Ingredients:

- 8 ounces ground beef (80% lean)
- 2 large eggs
- ½ cup shredded cheddar cheese
- Salt and pepper to taste
- 1 teaspoon olive oil
- 4 lettuce leaves
- 4 slices tomato

Instructions:

1. Mix together the beef, egg, cheddar cheese, salt and pepper in a bowl.
2. Divide the mixture in two and shape each into a patty.

3. Heat the olive oil in a skillet over medium-high heat.
4. Add the burgers and cook for 5 minutes on each side until cooked through.
5. Serve on a bed of lettuce and sliced tomato.

Nutrition: 500 calories, 40g fat, 32.5g protein, 2g net carbs

---

Lunch Recipes

Fried White Fish Cakes

Servings: 3

Serving Size: 3 patties

Prep Time: 25 minutes

Cook Time: 15 minutes

Ingredients:

- 1 small head cauliflower, chopped
- 2 tablespoons butter
- Salt and pepper to taste
- 12 ounces white fish fillets
- 2 tablespoons coconut oil
- ¼ cup almond flour
- 2 tablespoons ground flaxseed
- 1 large egg, whisked
- 2 green onions, sliced thin
- 2 tablespoons fresh chopped parsley
- 1 teaspoon fresh lemon zest

Instructions:

1. Place the cauliflower in a food processor and pulse into rice-like grains.
2. Melt the butter in a skillet over medium heat and add the cauliflower.
3. Cook for 30 seconds or so until fragrant then season with salt and pepper.
4. Let the cauliflower cook for 5 minutes or until tender then remove from heat.
5. Pat the fish dry with paper towel and season with salt and pepper.
6. Heat another skillet over medium-high heat and grease with coconut oil.
7. Add the fish and cook on one side for 2 to 3 minutes until seared.
8. Flip the fish and cook for another 2 to 3 minutes until just cooked through.
9. Flake the fish into a bowl then stir in the cauliflower and the remaining ingredients.
10. Shape the mixture into 9 even-sized patties.
11. Fry the fish cakes in olive oil until browned on both sides.
12. Whisk together the mayonnaise and garlic then serve with the fish cakes.

Nutrition: 430 calories, 30g fat, 33g protein, 3.5g net carbs

Dinner Recipes

Rosemary Apple Pork Tenderloin

Servings: 2

Serving Size: about ½ recipe

Prep Time: 10 minutes

Cook Time: 20 minutes

Ingredients:

- 1 tablespoon olive oil
- 2 (6-ounce) pork tenderloin chops
- Salt and pepper to taste
- ½ cup thinly sliced apple
- 2 teaspoons fresh chopped rosemary
- 2 cups chopped cauliflower
- 2 tablespoons butter
- 1 tablespoon fresh chopped parsley

Instructions:

1. Heat the oil in a skillet over medium-high heat and season the pork with salt and pepper.
2. Add the pork to the skillet and cook for 2 to 3 minutes on each side until seared.
3. Reduce the heat to low and add the apples and rosemary to the skillet.
4. Cover and cook on low heat for 8 minutes.
5. In a separate saucepan, bring some water to boil then add the cauliflower.
6. Cook for 2 to 3 minutes until tender, then drain and add to a food processor.

7. Add the butter and parsley and blend until smooth.
8. Serve the mashed cauliflower with the pork tenderloin (sliced).

Nutrition: 565 calories, 33g fat, 54g protein, 9.5g net carbs

---

Dinner Recipes

Enchilada Chicken Bake

Servings: 1

Serving Size: 1 recipe

Prep Time: 10 minutes

Cook Time: 1 hour

Ingredients:

- 2 bone-in chicken thighs
- Salt and pepper to taste
- ½ cup store-bought salsa
- 1 ounce shredded cheddar cheese
- 2 tablespoons sour cream
- 2 tablespoons diced avocado

Instructions:

1. Preheat the oven to 375°F and grease a small casserole dish with cooking spray.
2. Season the chicken with salt and pepper and place it in the dish.
3. Pour the salsa over top then sprinkle with cheese and cover with foil.

4. Bake for 45 to 60 minutes until the chicken is cooked through.
5. Top with sour cream and avocado to serve.

Nutrition: 580 calories, 43.5g fat, 39g protein, 4.5g net carbs

---

Dinner Recipes

Coconut Chicken Curry

Servings: 4

Serving Size: about ¼ recipe

Prep Time: 15 minutes

Cook Time: 30 minutes

Ingredients:

- 1 tablespoon olive oil
- 1 small yellow onion, chopped
- 1 ½ pounds boneless chicken thighs
- Salt and pepper to taste
- 1 (14-ounce) can coconut milk
- 1 tablespoon curry powder
- 1 teaspoon ground turmeric
- 2 cups fresh green beans, trimmed
- ¼ cup fresh chopped cilantro

Instructions:

1. Heat the oil in a deep skillet over medium heat.
2. Cook the onions in the oil for 5 minutes until translucent then remove to a bowl.
3. Reheat the skillet and add the chicken thighs – season with salt and pepper.
4. Cook for 4 to 5 minutes on each side until browned then remove.
5. Shred the chicken then add it to the deep skillet with the cooked onions.
6. Pour in the coconut milk and add the curry powder, turmeric and green beans.
7. Simmer for 20 minutes then garnish with fresh cilantro to serve.

Nutrition: 500 calories, 36g fat, 35.5g protein, 7g net carbs

---

Dinner Recipes

Pork-Stuffed Zucchini Boats

Servings: 1

Serving Size: 1 recipe

Prep Time: 10 minutes

Cook Time: 35 minutes

Ingredients:

- 1 medium zucchini
- 1 teaspoon olive oil
- 1 teaspoon butter

- 4 ounces ground pork
- ¼ cup diced yellow onion
- 1 clove garlic, minced
- ½ teaspoon ground cumin
- ¼ teaspoon chili powder
- Pinch onion powder
- Salt and pepper to taste
- ¼ cup shredded cheddar cheese

Instructions:

1. Preheat the oven to 400°F.
2. Cut the zucchini in half lengthwise, scoop out the middle and chop, leaving the halves.
3. Brush the zucchini halves with olive oil, then bake for 15 minutes.
4. Heat the butter in a skillet over medium heat, then add the chopped zucchini with the ground pork, onion, and garlic.
5. Cook until the pork is browned then stir in the seasonings and 2 tablespoons of cheese.
6. Spoon the mixture into the zucchini halves and place them on a baking sheet.
7. Sprinkle with the remaining cheese then bake for 20 minutes.

Nutrition: 570 calories, 41.5g fat, 39g protein, 8.5g net carbs

Dinner Recipes

Sausage and Cabbage Skillet

Servings: 4

Serving Size: about ¼ recipe

Prep Time: 10 minutes

Cook Time: 20 minutes

Ingredients:

- 5 large Italian sausage links
- 2 tablespoons butter
- 1 small head cabbage, sliced thin
- ½ cup sour cream
- Salt and pepper to taste

Instructions:

1. Heat a skillet over medium-high heat then add the sausage links.
2. Cook the sausages until browned, turning as needed, then remove and slice.
3. Reheat the skillet with the butter then add the cabbage.
4. Cook for 3 to 4 minutes until tender then stir in the sour cream and sliced sausage.
5. Season with salt and pepper then simmer for 10 minutes before serving.

Nutrition: 315 calories, 21g fat, 20g protein, 9.5g net carbs

Dinner Recipes

Pesto Grilled Pork Chops

Servings: 1

Serving Size: 1 recipe

Prep Time: 10 minutes

Cook Time: 25 minutes

Ingredients:

- 1 (5-ounce) pork loin chop
- 1 teaspoon olive oil
- Salt and pepper to taste
- 1 tablespoon melted butter
- 2 ounces fresh asparagus, trimmed

Instructions:

1. Brush the pork with olive oil and season with salt and pepper.
2. Preheat a grill pan to medium-high heat and grease with cooking spray.
3. Add the pork chop and grill for 10 minutes.
4. Flip the pork chop and grill for another 8 to 10 minutes until done.
5. Toss the asparagus with melted butter then grill until tender. Serve hot.

Nutrition: 590 calories, 50g fat, 32g protein, 1g net carbs

Dinner Recipes

Pan-Seared Lemon Rosemary Chicken

Servings: 2

Serving Size: 1 chicken breast, ½ cauliflower

Prep Time: 15 minutes

Cook Time: 20 minutes

Ingredients:

- 2 (6-ounce) chicken breasts
- Salt and pepper to taste
- 2 tablespoons fresh lemon juice
- 1 tablespoon fresh chopped rosemary
- 1 small head cauliflower, chopped
- 2 tablespoons butter

Instructions:

1. Place the chicken breasts on a piece of parchment and place another sheet over them.
2. Pound to about ½-inch thickness then season with salt and pepper.
3. Place the chicken breasts in a shallow dish and spritz with lemon juice.
4. Sprinkle with rosemary then let it rest for 1 hour at room temperature.
5. Heat a grill pan to medium-high and grease with cooking spray.
6. Cook the chicken breasts for about 7 minutes on each side until done.

7. Meanwhile, boil the cauliflower in salted water until tender.
8. Drain and transfer to a food processor and blend smooth with the butter.
9. Serve the chicken hot with the mashed cauliflower.

Nutrition: 465 calories, 24.5g fat, 52g protein, 4g net carbs

---

Dinner Recipes

Beef and Mushroom Stroganoff

Servings: 2

Serving Size: about ½ recipe

Prep Time: 10 minutes

Cook Time: 25 minutes

Ingredients:

- 1 tablespoon olive oil
- 1 small yellow onion, chopped
- 1 cup sliced mushrooms
- 8 ounces ground beef (80% lean)
- ½ cup sour cream
- 2 ounces blue cheese, crumbled
- ½ teaspoon dried thyme
- ¼ teaspoon dried oregano
- Salt and pepper to taste
- 2 medium zucchini

Instructions:

1. Heat the oil in a skillet over medium heat then add the onions.
2. Cook until the onions are browned, about 5 minutes.
3. Add the mushrooms and cook until they are browned then add the beef.
4. Cook the beef until done then drain some of the fat.
5. Stir in the sour cream, blue cheese, thyme, oregano, salt and pepper.
6. Simmer on low heat for 10 minutes until thick.
7. Slice the zucchinis into noodle-like threads then blanch in boiling water 1 minute.
8. Drain the zucchini and stir into the skillet mixture. Season to taste.

Nutrition: 625 calories, 51g fat, 31g protein, 11g net carbs

Dinner Recipes

Grilled Steak Kebabs

Servings: 1

Serving Size: 1 recipe

Prep Time: 10 minutes

Cook Time: 25 minutes

Ingredients:

- 1 tablespoon minced red onion
- ½ tablespoon fresh chopped cilantro
- 1 teaspoon fresh chopped parsley

- 1 clove garlic, minced
- 1 tablespoon olive oil
- 1 teaspoon white wine vinegar
- Salt and pepper to taste
- 4 ounces beef sirloin, cubed
- 1 small red pepper, cut into chunks

Instructions:

1. Combine the red onion, cilantro, parsley, and garlic in a mixing bowl.
2. Add the olive oil and vinegar then season with salt and pepper – toss well.
3. Preheat a grill pan to high heat and grease with cooking spray.
4. Season the beef with salt and pepper then slide onto skewers with red peppers.
5. Grill for 2 to 3 minutes on each side.
6. Serve the kebabs with the salsa spooned over top.

Nutrition: 365 calories, 21g fat, 34g protein, 9g net carbs

Dinner Recipes

Lamb Chops with Herb Butter

Servings: 2

Serving Size: about ½ recipe

Prep Time: 10 minutes

Cook Time: 25 minutes

Ingredients:

- ¼ cup butter, room temperature
- 2 cloves garlic, minced
- 1 tablespoon fresh chopped parsley
- 1 ½ teaspoon dried Italian seasoning
- 12 ounces bone-in lamb chops
- Salt and pepper to taste
- 1 tablespoon coconut oil
- 1 cup snap peas

Instructions:

1. Place the butter in a food processor with the garlic and herbs – pulse to combine.
2. Season the lamb with salt and pepper.
3. Heat the oil in a skillet over medium-high heat and add the chops.
4. Cook for 2 minutes until seared, then flip and cook for another 2 to 3 minutes.
5. Let the chops rest on a cutting board for 5 minutes.
6. Reheat the skillet and add the snap peas.
7. Sauté the peas with salt and pepper until tender, about 2 minutes.
8. Serve the lamb chops and snap peas topped with garlic herb butter.

Nutrition: 560 calories, 40g fat, 39g protein, 8g net carbs

Dinner Recipes

Cauliflower Fried Rice with Beef

Servings: 1

Serving Size: 1 recipe

Prep Time: 10 minutes

Cook Time: 20 minutes

Ingredients:

- 1 cup chopped cauliflower
- 2 teaspoons butter
- ½ small yellow onion, chopped
- 1 clove garlic, minced
- 1 teaspoon grated ginger
- ¼ cup diced red pepper
- 2 ounces ground beef (80% lean)
- 1 tablespoon soy sauce
- 2 teaspoons rice vinegar
- 1 teaspoon Sriracha
- 1 tablespoon coconut oil
- 2 large eggs

Instructions:

1. Place the cauliflower in a food processor and pulse into rice-like grains.
2. Heat the butter in a skillet over medium heat.
3. Add the onion, garlic, and ginger and cook for 2 minutes.
4. Stir in the red pepper and cook for another 5 minutes, stirring often.
5. Add the riced cauliflower and beef then cook until browned, about 4 to 5 minutes.
6. Stir in the soy sauce, rice vinegar, and Sriracha then push everything to the sides.
7. Melt the coconut oil in the middle of the skillet and crack the eggs into it.

8. Season with salt and pepper and cook to your preferred doneness.
9. Serve the fried rice with the fried eggs on top.

Nutrition: 550 calories, 43g fat, 26g protein, 12g net carbs

Dinner Recipes

Bacon-Wrapped Stuffed Meatballs

Servings: 3

Serving Size: 3 meatballs

Prep Time: 15 minutes

Cook Time: 25 minutes

Ingredients:

- 10 ounces ground beef (80% lean)
- 2 tablespoons almond flour
- Salt and pepper to taste
- ½ cup cream cheese, softened
- 1 tablespoon olive oil
- 9 slices bacon, halved lengthwise
- 1 tablespoon butter
- 3 cups cooked spaghetti squash
- 1 teaspoon dried parsley

Instructions:

1. Combine the ground beef with the almond flour, salt, and pepper.

2. Mix well then divide into 9 even-sized balls and flatten them slightly.
3. Spoon 2 or 3 teaspoons of cream cheese into the middle of each disc.
4. Fold the meat up around the cream cheese and shape into a ball.
5. Heat the oil in a large skillet over high heat.
6. Add the meatballs and cook for 2 minutes on each side until browned.
7. Wrap the meatballs in bacon and place them on a baking sheet.
8. Bake for 15 minutes at 350°F until the bacon is crisp.
9. Melt the butter in a skillet over medium heat and add the spaghetti squash.
10. Cook until the spaghetti squash is heated through then stir in the parsley.
11. Serve the spaghetti squash topped with the meatballs.

Nutrition: 575 calories, 41g fat, 43g protein, 8.5g net carbs

---

Dinner Recipes

Ribeye Steak with Green Beans

Servings: 2

Serving Size: 1 steak

Prep Time: 10 minutes

Cook Time: 1 hour

Ingredients:

- 2 (5-ounce) ribeye steaks

- Salt and pepper to taste
- 1 tablespoon butter
- 2 cups trimmed green beans
- 2 cloves garlic, minced
- 1 tablespoon fresh lemon juice

Instructions:

1. Preheat the oven to 250°F.
2. Place a wire rack over a cookie sheet and place the steaks on top.
3. Season with salt and pepper then bake for 45 minutes.
4. Heat the butter in a large heavy skillet over high heat.
5. Add the steaks and cook for 30 to 45 seconds on each side to sear.
6. Remove the steaks to a cutting board and add the green beans to the skillet.
7. Add the garlic and lemon juice then sauté for 5 minutes until tender.
8. Slice the steaks and serve with the green beans.

Nutrition: 475 calories, 36g fat, 27g protein, 5g net carbs

Dinner Recipes

Cauliflower and Steak Skillet

Servings: 2

Serving Size: about ½ recipe

Prep Time: 10 minutes

Cook Time: 25 minutes

Ingredients:

- 2 tablespoons butter
- 1 small head cauliflower, chopped
- 6 ounces beef sirloin, chopped
- Salt and pepper to taste
- 2 ounces shredded cheddar cheese
- ¼ cup sour cream

Instructions:

1. Heat the butter in a cast-iron skillet over medium-high heat.
2. Add the cauliflower and sauté for 5 minutes until browned.
3. Toss in the steak and season with salt and pepper.
4. Cook for 5 to 7 minutes until the steak is browned and cooked through.
5. Spread the ingredients evenly in the skillet then top with cheese.
6. Bake at 400°F for 10 minutes to melt the cheese. Serve with sour cream.

Nutrition: 405 calories, 25g fat, 36.5g protein, 5.5g net carbs

---

Dinner Recipes

Broccoli Cheddar Casserole with Lamb

Servings: 4

Serving Size: about ¼ recipe

Prep Time: 15 minutes

Cook Time: 35 minutes

Ingredients:

- 1 pound ground lamb
- 1 pound fresh chopped broccoli florets
- 1 ½ cups shredded cheddar cheese
- 4 slices bacon, cooked and chopped
- ½ cup cream cheese, at room temperature
- 6 tablespoons sour cream
- Salt and pepper to taste

Instructions:

1. Preheat the oven to 350°F and grease a square glass baking dish.
2. Cook the lamb in a skillet over medium-high heat until browned.
3. Transfer the lamb to a large bowl with the broccoli, 1 cup cheese, and half the chopped bacon.
4. Beat together the cream cheese, sour cream, salt and pepper.
5. Toss the lamb and broccoli with the cream cheese mixture and spread in the dish.
6. Sprinkle with the rest of the cheese and bacon then bake for 35 minutes.

Nutrition: 610 calories, 40.5g fat, 52g protein, 5.5g net carbs

Dinner Recipes

Shrimp Zoodle Alfredo

Servings: 3

Serving Size: about ⅓ recipe

Prep Time: 15 minutes

Cook Time: 20 minutes

Ingredients:

- 3 medium zucchini
- 2 tablespoons olive oil
- 3 cloves garlic, minced
- 1 tablespoon pine nuts
- 2 cups unsweetened almond milk
- ¼ cup nutritional yeast
- 1 tablespoon fresh lemon juice
- 1 tablespoon butter
- 12 ounces large shrimp, peeled and deveined

Instructions:

1. Peel the zucchini with a spiralizer then spread in a colander and sprinkle with salt.
2. Let the zucchini drain for 15 minutes then rinse and wring out as much moisture as possible.
3. Heat the oil in a saucepan over medium heat then add the garlic and pine nuts.
4. Cook for 3 minutes until browned then stir in the almond milk.
5. Bring to a boil then stir in the cauliflower and spices and simmer for 10 minutes.

6. Transfer the mixture to a food processor and blend until smooth with the nutritional yeast and lemon juice.
7. Heat the butter in a skillet over medium-high heat.
8. Add the shrimp and season with salt and pepper then cook until just opaque.
9. Toss in the zucchini noodles and Alfredo sauce, and cook until heated through.

Nutrition: 335 calories, 18.5g fat, 31g protein, 11g net carbs

---

Dinner Recipes

Seared Salmon with Sautéed Kale

Servings: 2

Serving Size: 1 fillet with ½ spinach

Prep Time: 10 minutes

Cook Time: 20 minutes

Ingredients:

- 1 tablespoon olive oil
- 8 ounces sliced mushrooms
- 1 small yellow onion, chopped
- 1 tablespoon minced garlic
- ½ tablespoon grated ginger
- 1 small tomato, diced
- 2 tablespoons butter
- 2 (6-ounce) salmon fillets
- 2 cups fresh chopped kale

Instructions:

1. Heat the oil in a large skillet over medium heat.
2. Add the mushrooms, onion, garlic, and ginger and season with salt and pepper.
3. Cook for 3 to 4 minutes until the mushrooms start to brown.
4. Stir in the tomatoes and cook for 2 minutes then add the butter.
5. Push the vegetables to the sides of the skillet.
6. Add the salmon fillets and cook for 4 minutes until seared.
7. Flip the salmon and cook until seared on the other side.
8. Remove the salmon then add the kale and cook until wilted.
9. Toss the kale with lemon juice, salt, and pepper then serve with the salmon.

Nutrition: 475 calories, 29.5g fat, 40g protein, 14g net carbs

---

Dinner Recipes

Parmesan Crusted Halibut

Servings: 4

Serving Size: 1 fillet

Prep Time: 10 minutes

Cook Time: 15 minutes

Ingredients:

- 4 tablespoons butter, softened
- 2 tablespoons grated parmesan
- 1 tablespoon almond flour
- 1 teaspoon garlic powder
- 4 (6-ounce) halibut fillets
- Salt and pepper to taste
- 8 ounces fresh asparagus, trimmed
- 1 tablespoon olive oil

Instructions:

1. Preheat the oven to 400°F and line a baking sheet with foil.
2. Combine the butter, parmesan, almond flour, and garlic powder in a blender and blend until smooth.
3. Pat the halibut dry with paper towels, then season with salt and pepper.
4. Place the fillets on the baking sheet and spoon the parmesan mixture over them.
5. Toss the asparagus with olive oil and season with salt and pepper.
6. Place the asparagus on the baking sheet with the fish.
7. Bake for 10 to 12 minutes until the fish is almost cooked through.
8. Broil for 2 to 3 minutes until the topping is golden brown. Serve hot.

Nutrition: 565 calories, 46g fat, 34g protein, 1.5g net carbs

Dinner Recipes

Dijon-Baked Salmon

Servings: 2

Serving Size: 1 fillet and ½ asparagus

Prep Time: 15 minutes

Cook Time: 15 minutes

Ingredients:

- 3 tablespoons Dijon mustard
- 2 (6-ounce) salmon fillets
- Salt and pepper to taste
- 1 ounce pork rinds
- 16 asparagus spears, trimmed

Instructions:

- Preheat the oven to 400°F.
- Season the fillets with salt and pepper then brush with mustard.
- Crush up the pork rinds in a plastic bag, then sprinkle over the salmon.
- Drizzle the asparagus with oil and toss to coat.
- Place the salmon on a foil-lined baking sheet with the asparagus and bake for 15 minutes. Serve hot.

Nutrition: 365 calories, 18g fat, 48g protein, 2.5g net carbs

Dinner Recipes

<u>Broccoli White Fish Casserole</u>

Servings: 4

Serving Size: about ¼ recipe

Prep Time: 15 minutes

Cook Time: 20 minutes

Ingredients:

- 1 tablespoon olive oil
- 1 pound fresh chopped broccoli
- 4 tablespoons butter, softened
- 5 scallions, sliced thin
- 2 tablespoons capers, drained
- 1 ½ pounds white fish fillets (3 to 4 ounces each)
- 1 ¼ cups heavy cream
- 1 tablespoon Dijon mustard
- 2 tablespoons fresh chopped parsley
- 6 cups fresh spring greens
- ½ cup sliced mushrooms
- ½ cup diced red pepper
- ¼ cup extra-virgin olive oil
- 2 tablespoons balsamic vinegar
- 1 teaspoon powdered erythritol
- Salt and pepper to taste

Instructions:

1. Preheat the oven to 400°F.
2. Heat the oil in a skillet over medium-high heat then add the broccoli.

3. Sauté the broccoli for 5 minutes then season with salt and pepper.
4. Stir in the scallions and capers and cook for another 2 minutes, stirring often.
5. Spoon the mixture into a casserole dish and place the fish on top.
6. Whisk together the heavy cream, mustard, and parsley then pour over top.
7. Spread the butter over the casserole and bake for 20 minutes.
8. Toss together the remaining ingredients and serve the spring greens with the casserole.

Nutrition: 640 calories, 45g fat, 48g protein, 8.5g net carbs

---

Dinner Recipes

Shrimp Scampi with Spaghetti Squash

Servings: 4

Serving Size: about ¼ recipe

Prep Time: 5 minutes

Cook Time: 15 minutes

Ingredients:

- 3 tablespoons olive oil
- 2 tablespoons butter
- 2 cups cooked spaghetti squash
- 3 cloves garlic, minced
- ½ cup dry white wine
- Salt and pepper to taste

- 1 ½ pounds large shrimp, peeled and deveined
- ¼ cup fresh chopped parsley
- 1 tablespoon fresh lemon juice

Instructions:

1. Heat the oil and butter together in a skillet.
2. Add the spaghetti squash and garlic and cook for 2 minutes, then stir in the wine, seasoning with salt and pepper.
3. Cook for 2 minutes then add the shrimp and cook until opaque, about 3 minutes.
4. Remove from heat and stir in the parsley and lemon juice. Serve hot.

Nutrition: 325 calories, 16.5g fat, 32.5g protein, 8g net carbs

Snack Recipes

Guacamole Deviled Eggs

Servings: 4

Serving Size: 4 pieces

Prep Time: 15 minutes

Cook Time: 0 minutes

Ingredients:

- 8 large eggs
- ½ cup chopped avocado
- 2 tablespoons canned coconut milk
- 1 tablespoon chopped cilantro
- 1 teaspoon fresh lime juice
- ¼ teaspoon ground cumin
- Salt and pepper to taste
- Paprika for garnish

Instructions:

1. Place the eggs in a saucepan and cover with water.
2. Bring the water to a boil, then remove from heat and let rest for 10 minutes.
3. Rinse the eggs in cold water until cool enough to handle, then peel.
4. Cut the eggs in half and spoon the yolks into a bowl.
5. Add the avocado, coconut milk, cilantro, lime juice, and cumin.
6. Season with salt and pepper and stir until smooth.
7. Spoon or pipe the mixture into the egg halves then sprinkle with paprika.

Nutrition:185 calories, 15g fat, 12g protein, 2g net carbs

Snack Recipes

<u>Curry Spiced Almonds</u>

Servings: 4

Serving Size: about ¼ cup

Prep Time: 5 minutes

Cook Time: 25 minutes

Ingredients:

- 1 cup whole almonds
- 2 teaspoons olive oil
- 1 teaspoon curry powder
- ¼ teaspoon salt
- ¼ teaspoon ground turmeric
- Pinch cayenne

Instructions:

1. Preheat the oven to 300°F and line a baking sheet with foil.
2. In a mixing bowl, whisk together the olive oil and spices.
3. Toss in the almonds then spread on the baking sheet.
4. Bake for 25 minutes until toasted, then cool and store in an airtight container.

Nutrition: 155 calories, 14g fat, 5g protein, 2g net carbs

Snack Recipes

Chia Peanut Butter Bites

Servings: 6

Serving Size: 1 square

Prep Time: 10 minutes

Cook Time: 10 minutes

Ingredients:

- ½ ounce raw almonds
- 1 tablespoon powdered erythritol
- 4 teaspoons coconut oil
- 2 tablespoons canned coconut milk
- ½ teaspoon vanilla extract
- 2 tablespoons chia seeds, ground to powder
- ¼ cup coconut cream

Instructions:

1. Place the almonds in a skillet over medium-low heat, and cook until toasted, takes about 5 minutes.
2. Transfer the almonds to a food processor with the erythritol and 1 teaspoon coconut oil.
3. Blend until it forms a smooth almond butter.
4. Heat the rest of the coconut oil in a skillet over medium heat.
5. Add the coconut milk and vanilla and bring to a simmer.
6. Stir in the ground chia seeds, coconut cream, and almond butter.

7. Cook for 2 minutes then spread in a foil-lined square dish.
8. Chill until the mixture is firm then cut into squares to serve.

Nutrition: 110 calories, 8g fat, 2g protein, 7g net carbs

Snack Recipes

<u>Cheesy Sausage Dip</u>

Servings: 12

Serving Size: about ¼ cup

Prep Time: 10 minutes

Cook Time: 2 hours

Ingredients:

- ½ pound ground Italian sausage
- ½ cup diced tomatoes
- 2 green onions, sliced thin
- 4 ounces cream cheese, cubed
- 4 ounces pepper jack cheese, cubed
- 1 cup sour cream

Instructions:

1. Brown the sausage in a skillet until cooked through then stir in the tomatoes.
2. Cook for 2 minutes, stirring often, then stir in the green onions.

3. Line the bottom of a slow cooker with the cheeses then spoon the sausage mixture on top.
4. Spoon the sour cream over the sausage, then cover and cook on high heat for 2 hours, stirring once halfway through.
5. Serve with celery sticks or pork rinds for dipping.

Nutrition: 170 calories, 15g fat, 7g protein, 2g net carbs

Snack Recipes

Salted Kale Chips

Servings: 2

Serving Size: ½ recipe

Prep Time: 10 minutes

Cook Time: 12 minutes

Ingredients:

- ½ bunch fresh kale
- 1 tablespoon olive oil
- Salt and pepper to taste

Instructions:

1. Preheat the oven to 350°F and line a baking sheet with foil.
2. Trim the thick stems from the kale and then tear the leaves into pieces.
3. Toss the kale with olive oil and spread on the baking sheet.

4. Bake for 10 to 12 minutes until crisp then sprinkle with salt and pepper.

Nutrition: 75 calories, 7g fat, 1g protein, 3g net carbs

Snack Recipes

Bacon Jalapeno Quick Bread

Servings: 10

Serving Size: 1 slice

Prep Time: 20 minutes

Cook Time: 45 minutes

Ingredients:

- 4 slices thick-cut bacon
- 3 jalapeno peppers
- ½ cup coconut flour, sifted
- ½ teaspoon baking soda
- ½ teaspoon salt
- 6 large eggs, beaten
- ½ cup coconut oil, melted
- ¼ cup water

Instructions:

1. Preheat the oven to 400°F and grease a loaf pan with cooking spray.
2. Spread the bacon and jalapenos on a baking sheet and roast for 10 minutes, stirring halfway through.

3. Crumble the bacon and cut the jalapenos in half to remove the seeds.
4. Combine the bacon and jalapeno in a food processor and pulse until well chopped.
5. Whisk together the coconut flour, baking soda, and salt in a bowl.
6. Add the eggs, coconut oil, and water then stir in the bacon and jalapenos.
7. Spread in the loaf pan and bake for 40 to 45 minutes until a knife inserted in the center comes out clean.

Nutrition: 225 calories, 19g fat, 8g protein, 3g net carbs

Snack Recipes

Toasted Pumpkin Seeds

Servings: 4

Serving Size: about 2 tablespoons

Prep Time: 5 minutes

Cook Time: 5 minutes

Ingredients:

- ½ cup hulled pumpkin seeds
- 2 teaspoons coconut oil
- 2 teaspoons chili powder
- ½ teaspoon salt

Instructions:

1. Heat up a cast-iron skillet over medium heat.

2. Add the pumpkin seeds and let them cook until toasted, about 3 to 5 minutes, stirring often.
3. Remove from heat and stir in the coconut oil, chili powder, and salt.
4. Let the seeds cool then store in an airtight container.

Nutrition: 100 calories, 8.5g fat, 5.5g protein, 0.5g net carbs

---

Snack Recipes

Bacon-Wrapped Burger Bites

Servings: 6

Serving Size: 1 piece

Prep Time: 5 minutes

Cook Time: 60 minutes

Ingredients:

- 6 ounces ground beef (80% lean)
- ¼ teaspoon onion powder
- ¼ teaspoon garlic powder
- ¼ teaspoon ground cumin
- Salt and pepper to taste
- 6 slices bacon, uncooked

Instructions:

1. Preheat the oven to 350°F and line a baking sheet with foil.

2. Combine the onion powder, garlic powder, cumin, salt and pepper in a bowl.
3. Add the beef and stir until well combined.
4. Divide the ground beef mixture into 6 even portions and roll them into balls.
5. Wrap each ball in a slice of bacon and place on the baking sheet.
6. Bake for 50 to 60 minutes until the bacon is crisp and the beef is cooked through.

Nutrition: 150 calories, 10g fat, 16g protein, 0.5g net carbs

---

Snack Recipes

<u>Almond Sesame Crackers</u>

Servings: 6

Serving Size: 5 to 6 crackers

Prep Time: 10 minutes

Cook Time: 15 minutes

Ingredients:

- 1 ½ cups almond flour
- ½ cup sesame seeds
- 1 teaspoon dried oregano
- ½ teaspoon salt
- 1 large egg, whisked
- 1 tablespoon coconut oil, melted

Instructions:

1. Preheat the oven to 350°F and line a baking sheet with parchment.
2. Whisk together the almond flour, sesame seeds, oregano, and salt in a bowl.
3. Add the eggs and coconut oil, stirring into a soft dough.
4. Sandwich the dough between two sheets of parchment and roll to ⅛ thickness.
5. Cut into squares and arrange on the baking sheet.
6. Bake for 10 to 12 minutes until browned around the edges.

Nutrition: 145 calories, 12.5g fat, 5g protein, 2g net carbs

Snack Recipes

<u>Cauliflower Cheese Dip</u>

Servings: 6

Serving Size: about ¼ cup

Prep Time: 5 minutes

Cook Time: 15 minutes

Ingredients:

-   1 small head cauliflower, chopped
-   ¾ cup chicken broth
-   ¼ teaspoon ground cumin
-   ¼ teaspoon chili powder
-   ¼ teaspoon garlic powder

- Salt and pepper to taste
- ⅓ cup cream cheese, chopped
- 2 tablespoons canned coconut milk

Instructions:

1. Combine the cauliflower and chicken broth in a saucepan and simmer until the cauliflower is tender.
2. Add the cumin, chili powder, and garlic powder then season with salt and pepper.
3. Stir in the cream cheese until melted, then blend everything with an immersion blender.
4. Whisk in the coconut milk then spoon into a serving bowl.
5. Serve with sliced celery sticks.

Nutrition: 75 calories, 6g fat, 2.5g protein, 2g net carbs

Snack Recipes

Deviled Eggs with Bacon

Servings: 6

Serving Size: 2 pieces

Prep Time: 20 minutes

Cook Time: 0 minutes

Ingredients:

- 6 large eggs
- 3 slices thick-cut bacon
- ¼ cup avocado oil mayonnaise

- 1 teaspoon Dijon mustard

Instructions:

1. Place the eggs in a saucepan and cover with water.
2. Bring the water to boil then remove from heat and let rest for 10 minutes.
3. Meanwhile, cook the bacon in a skillet over medium-high heat until crisp.
4. Rinse the eggs in cold water until cool enough to handle, then peel them.
5. Cut the eggs in half and spoon the yolks into a bowl.
6. Add 1 tablespoon of bacon fat from the skillet along with the mayonnaise and mustard.
7. Spoon the mixture into the egg halves then crumble the bacon over top.

Nutrition: 145 calories, 11g fat, 8.5g protein, 3g net carbs

Snack Recipes

Coleslaw with Avocado Dressing

Servings: 6

Serving Size: about ½ cup

Prep Time: 15 minutes

Cook Time: 0 minutes

Ingredients:

- 1 small head green cabbage, sliced thin
- ½ cup shredded red cabbage

- 1 small red pepper, diced
- 1 cup avocado oil
- 1 large egg, beaten
- Juice from 1 lime
- 1 clove garlic, minced
- Salt to taste

Instructions:

1. Combine the shredded cabbages with the red peppers in a bowl.
2. Place the avocado oil, egg, lime juice, and garlic in a blender.
3. Blend smooth then season with salt to taste.
4. Toss the dressing with the salad and chill until ready to serve.

Nutrition: 100 calories, 6g fat, 3g protein, 6g net carbs

Snack Recipes

Creamsicle Fat Bombs

Servings: 10

Serving Size: 1 fat bomb

Prep Time: 5 minutes

Cook Time: 0 minutes

Ingredients:

- 4 ounces cream cheese, softened
- ½ cup heavy cream

- ½ cup coconut oil
- 1 teaspoon orange extract
- 8 to 12 drops liquid stevia extract

Instructions:

1. Combine the cream cheese, heavy cream, and coconut oil in a bowl.
2. Blend with an immersion blender until smooth – microwave if needed to soften.
3. Stir in the orange extract and liquid stevia.
4. Spoon the mixture into silicone molds and freeze for 3 hours until solid.
5. Remove the fat bombs from the mold and store in the freezer.

Nutrition: 155 calories, 17g fat, 1g protein, 0.5g net carbs

Snack Recipes

Baked Cauliflower Bites

Servings: 4

Serving Size: ¼ recipe

Prep Time: 15 minutes

Cook Time: 25 minutes

Ingredients:

- 1 small head cauliflower, chopped
- ¼ cup coconut flour
- 2 large eggs

- ½ teaspoon garlic powder
- ¼ teaspoon onion powder
- Salt and pepper to taste

Instructions:

1. Preheat the oven to 400°F and line a baking sheet with foil.
2. Place the cauliflower in a saucepan and cover with water.
3. Boil until the cauliflower is tender then drain and place in a food processor.
4. Pulse into rice-like grains then pulse in the rest of the ingredients.
5. Drop the mixture onto the baking sheet in rounded spoonfuls.
6. Bake for 20 to 25 minutes until browned, flipping once halfway through.

Nutrition: 100 calories, 4.5g fat, 6g protein, 4g net carbs

Snack Recipes

Bacon-Wrapped Shrimp

Servings: 4

Serving Size: 3 shrimp

Prep Time: 10 minutes

Cook Time: 15 minutes

Ingredients:

- 6 slices uncooked bacon
- 12 large shrimp, peeled and deveined
- Paprika to taste
- Salt and pepper

Instructions:

1. Preheat the oven to 425°F and line a baking sheet with foil.
2. Cut the slices of bacon in half, then wrap one piece around each shrimp.
3. Place the shrimp on the baking sheet and sprinkle with paprika, salt and pepper.
4. Spray lightly with cooking spray then bake for 15 minutes until bacon is crisp.

Nutrition: 100 calories, 6g fat, 9g protein, 0.5g net carbs

Snack Recipes

Macadamia Blueberry Squares

Servings: 16

Serving Size: 1 square

Prep Time: 10 minutes

Cook Time: 0 minutes

Ingredients:

- 1 ounce macadamia nuts
- ¼ cup canned coconut milk solids (liquid drained)
- ½ cup coconut butter

- ½ cup coconut oil
- ½ cup fresh blueberries
- ½ teaspoon vanilla extract
- Liquid stevia extract to taste

Instructions:

1. Preheat the oven to 325°F and line a small glass dish with foil.
2. Place the nuts in a food processor and pulse into a ground mixture.
3. Spread the ground nuts in the baking dish and bake for 5 to 6 minutes until browned slightly.
4. Beat the coconut milk until light and fluffy then spread in the dish.
5. Add the rest of the ingredients to the food processor and blend until smooth.
6. Spread the mixture in the baking dish and freeze for 60 minutes until firm.
7. Cut the mixture into squares to serve.

Nutrition: 175 calories, 18g fat, 1g protein, 2g net carbs

Snack Recipes

Pepperoni Pizza Dip

Servings: 4

Serving Size: 1 ramekin

Prep Time: 5 minutes

Cook Time: 20 minutes

Ingredients:

- 4 ounces cream cheese, room temperature
- ¼ cup sour cream
- ¼ cup mayonnaise
- 1 cup shredded mozzarella cheese
- Salt and pepper to taste
- ½ cup low-carb tomato sauce
- 2 ounces pepperoni, diced
- ½ cup diced mushrooms
- ¼ cup diced yellow onion

Instructions:

1. Preheat the oven to 350°F and lightly grease four ramekins with cooking spray.
2. Place the cream cheese in a bowl and stir in the sour cream, mayonnaise, and mozzarella.
3. Season with salt and pepper then spoon into the ramekins.
4. Top with tomato sauce, diced pepperoni, mushrooms, and onions.
5. Sprinkle with parmesan cheese then bake for 18 to 20 minutes until bubbly.
6. Serve with celery sticks or keto-friendly crackers.

Nutrition: 290 calories, 26g fat, 8.5g protein, 6.5g net carbs

Snack Recipes

Chia Coconut Bites

Servings: 8

Serving Size: 1 bite

Prep Time: 5 minutes

Cook Time: 0 minutes

Ingredients:

- ½ cup coconut oil
- ¼ cup chia seeds
- ¼ cup shredded unsweetened coconut
- ½ teaspoon vanilla
- Liquid stevia extract

Instructions:

1. Combine the coconut oil, chia seeds, coconut, vanilla, and stevia in a food processor.
2. Blend the mixture until well combined, then roll into 8 balls.
3. Freeze until solid then serve the bites cold.

Nutrition: 160 calories, 16.5g fat, 1.5g protein, 0.5g net carbs

Snack Recipes

<u>Lemon Blueberry Snack Bread</u>

Servings: 10

Serving Size: 1 slice

Prep Time: 10 minutes

Cook Time: 60 minutes

Ingredients:

- 3 cups almond flour
- 1 scoop whey protein powder
- 1 teaspoon cream of tartar
- ½ teaspoon baking soda
- ¼ teaspoon salt
- 6 large eggs
- 2 tablespoons fresh lemon zest
- ½ teaspoon vanilla extract
- ¼ teaspoon liquid stevia extract
- 1 cup fresh blueberries

Instructions:

1. Preheat the oven to 350°F and grease a loaf pan.
2. Whisk together the almond flour, protein powder, cream of tartar, baking soda, and salt in a mixing bowl.
3. In a separate bowl, whisk together the eggs, lemon zest, liquid stevia, and vanilla extract.
4. Whisk the wet ingredients into the dry then fold in the blueberries.

5. Spread evenly in the loaf pan and bake for 45 to 60 minutes until a knife inserted in the center comes out clean.
6. Let the bread cool completely then slice to serve.

Nutrition: 165 calories, 11g fat, 10g protein, 4.5g net carbs

---

Snack Recipes

Cocoa Chocolate Fat Bombs

Servings: 6

Serving Size: 1 fat bomb

Prep Time: 10 minutes

Cook Time: 0 minutes

Ingredients:

- ¼ cup coconut oil
- ¼ cup canned coconut milk
- 1 tablespoon unsweetened cocoa powder
- 2 teaspoons powdered erythritol
- ¼ teaspoon vanilla extract

Instructions:

1. Combine the coconut oil, coconut milk, cocoa powder, erythritol, and vanilla in a food processor.
2. Blend the mixture until smooth and well combined.
3. Spoon into a silicone mold or shape into balls by hand.
4. Freeze the fat bombs until solid then enjoy cold.

Nutrition: 100 calories, 11g fat, 0.5g protein, 0.5g net carbs

---

Snack Recipes

Pepperoni Pizza Chips

Servings: 6

Serving Size: 3 to 4 chips

Prep Time: 5 minutes

Cook Time: 10 minutes

Ingredients:

- 6 ounces sliced pepperoni
- 4 ounces shredded mozzarella cheese

Instructions:

1. Preheat the oven to 400°F.
2. Arrange the sliced pepperoni in batches of four, overlapping slightly, to make the "chips".
3. Bake for 5 minutes until they just start to crisp around the edges.
4. Sprinkle with cheese and bake for another 3 to 4 minutes until the cheese is melted and crisp.
5. Drain on paper towels, then serve.

Nutrition: 190 calories, 16g fat, 12g protein, 0.5g net carbs

Dessert and Drinks Recipes

Coconut Chia Pudding

Servings: 8

Serving Size: about ½ cup

Prep Time: 35 minutes

Cook Time: 0 minutes

Ingredients:

- 2 ¼ cup canned coconut milk
- 2 tablespoons powdered erythritol
- 1 teaspoon vanilla extract
- ½ cup chia seeds
- Pinch salt

Instructions:

1. Combine the coconut milk, erythritol, and vanilla in a bowl.
2. Whisk in the chia seeds and salt.
3. Let rest for at least 30 minutes, chill if left overnight.
4. Spoon into cups and top with whipped cream to serve.

Nutrition: 225 calories, 20.5g fat, 4.5g protein, 3g net carbs

Dessert and Drinks Recipes

<u>Banana Lime Smoothie</u>

Servings: 2

Serving Size: ½ recipe

Prep Time: 5 minutes

Cook Time: 0 minutes

Ingredients:

- ½ cup canned coconut milk
- ½ cup unsweetened almond milk
- 2 tablespoons fresh lime juice
- 2 tablespoons ground flaxseed
- 1 teaspoon coconut oil
- ¼ teaspoon banana extract
- Ice cubes, optional
- ¼ cup whipped cream

Instructions:

1. Combine all of the ingredients in a blender.
2. Pulse several times, then blend for 30 to 60 seconds.
3. Add ice to thicken, if desired, and blend until smooth.
4. Pour into two glasses and top with whipped cream to serve.

Nutrition: 250 calories, 24g fat, 3g protein, 3g net carbs

Dessert and Drinks Recipes

Almond Cinnamon Bars

Servings: 6

Serving Size: 1 bar

Prep Time: 30 minutes

Cook Time: 0 minutes

Ingredients:

- 1 cup coconut cream
- 1 ½ teaspoons ground cinnamon, divided
- 2 tablespoons almond butter
- 4 tablespoons coconut oil, divided

Instructions:

1. Line a regular loaf pan with waxed paper and set aside.
2. Combine the coconut cream with ¼ teaspoon cinnamon in a bowl.
3. Stir smooth then spread in the bottom of the loaf pan.
4. In a mixing bowl, whisk together the almond butter and 2 tablespoons coconut oil then spread in the loaf pan.
5. Combine the rest of the coconut oil and cinnamon then spoon into a sandwich bag.
6. Snip the corner and drizzle the mixture into the loaf pan.
7. Freeze the mixture until firm then cut into 6 bars.

Nutrition: 200 calories, 22g fat, 2g protein, 2g net carbs

Dessert and Drinks Recipes

Vanilla Almond Butter Smoothie

Servings: 2

Serving Size: ½ recipe

Prep Time: 5 minutes

Cook Time: 0 minutes

Ingredients:

- 1 cup unsweetened almond milk
- ¼ cup full-fat Greek yogurt
- 1 scoop vanilla whey protein powder
- 2 tablespoons almond butter
- 1 teaspoon vanilla extract
- Liquid stevia, to taste
- Ice cubes, optional
- ¼ cup whipped cream

Instructions:

1. Combine all of the ingredients in a blender.
2. Pulse several times, then blend for 30 to 60 seconds.
3. Add ice to thicken, if desired, and blend until smooth.
4. Pour into two glasses and top with whipped cream to serve.

Nutrition: 240 calories, 16.5g fat, 16g protein, 4.5g net carbs

Dessert and Drinks Recipes

Sweet Cinnamon Bread

Servings: 10

Serving Size: 1 slice

Prep Time: 20 minutes

Cook Time: 30 minutes

Ingredients:

- ½ cup coconut flour, sifted
- 2 teaspoons ground cinnamon
- 1 teaspoon baking soda
- ¼ teaspoon baking powder
- Pinch salt
- 3 large eggs
- 6 tablespoons canned coconut milk
- 3 tablespoons coconut oil
- 2 tablespoons water
- 1 teaspoon distilled white vinegar
- 1 tablespoon powdered Erythritol sweetener, or to taste

Instructions:

1. Preheat the oven to 350°F and grease a loaf pan.
2. Whisk together the dry ingredients in a mixing bowl.
3. In a separate bowl, whisk together the eggs, coconut milk, coconut oil, water, and vinegar.
4. Stir in the sweetener and let the mixture rest for 5 to 10 minutes.

5. Spread in the loaf pan and bake for 25 to 30 minutes until a knife inserted in the center comes out clean.
6. Let the bread cool completely then slice to serve.

Nutrition: 155 calories, 12g fat, 4.5g protein, 4g net carbs

Dessert and Drinks Recipes

Chocolate Protein Smoothie

Servings: 2

Serving Size: ½ recipe

Prep Time: 5 minutes

Cook Time: 0 minutes

Ingredients:

- 1 cup unsweetened almond milk
- 2 scoops chocolate whey protein powder
- ¼ cup full-fat Greek yogurt
- 1 tablespoon unsweetened cocoa powder
- ½ teaspoon vanilla extract
- Ice cubes, optional
- ¼ cup whipped cream

Instructions:

1. Combine all of the ingredients in a blender.
2. Pulse several times, then blend for 30 to 60 seconds.
3. Add ice to thicken, if desired, and blend until smooth.
4. Pour into two glasses and top with whipped cream to serve.

Nutrition: 150 calories, 8.5g fat, 12g protein, 6g net carbs

Dessert and Drinks Recipes

Lemon Poppy Ice Cream

Servings: 12

Serving Size: about ½ cup

Prep Time: 15 minutes

Cook Time: 0 minutes

Ingredients:

- ¼ cup chia seeds
- 3 tablespoons poppy seeds
- 3 cups canned coconut milk
- Juice from 2 lemons
- ¼ cup powdered erythritol
- ¼ cup coconut oil

Instructions:

1. Place the chia seeds and poppy seeds in a spice grinder and grind into powder.
2. Pour the coconut milk into a bowl and whisk in the powder, then let rest 5 minutes.
3. Combine the rest of the ingredients in a blender, then add the chia mixture.
4. Blend smooth, then pour into a rectangular Tupperware container.
5. Freeze the mixture until solid, then break into pieces and blend smooth to serve.

Nutrition: 215 calories, 21g fat, 3g protein, 2.5g net carbs

Dessert and Drinks Recipes

Strawberry Lemon Smoothie

Servings: 2

Serving Size: ½ recipe

Prep Time: 5 minutes

Cook Time: 0 minutes

Ingredients:

- 1 cup unsweetened almond milk
- ½ cup full-fat Greek yogurt
- 5 frozen strawberries
- 2 tablespoons fresh lemon juice
- 1 teaspoon coconut oil
- Ice cubes, optional
- ¼ cup whipped cream

Instructions:

1. Combine all of the ingredients in a blender.
2. Pulse several times, then blend for 30 to 60 seconds.
3. Add ice to thicken, if desired, and blend until smooth.
4. Pour into two glasses and top with whipped cream to serve.

Nutrition: 145 calories, 11g fat, 2.5g protein, 8g net carbs

Dessert and Drinks Recipes

Vanilla White Chocolate Fat Bombs

Servings: 8

Serving Size: 1 fat bomb

Prep Time: 10 minutes

Cook Time: 0 minutes

Ingredients:

- ¼ cup cocoa butter
- ¼ cup coconut oil
- ¼ teaspoon vanilla extract
- 8 to 10 drops liquid stevia extract

Instructions:

1. Combine the cocoa butter and coconut oil in a double boiler over low heat.
2. Heat until the ingredients are melted, then remove from heat.
3. Stir in the vanilla extract and stevia, then pour into 8 silicone molds.
4. Chill until hardened, then remove from the molds and enjoy.

Nutrition: 120 calories, 14g fat, 0g protein, 0g net carbs

Dessert and Drinks Recipes

Creamy Avocado Smoothie

Servings: 2

Serving Size: ½ recipe

Prep Time: 5 minutes

Cook Time: 0 minutes

Ingredients:

- 1 cup unsweetened almond milk
- ½ cup canned coconut milk
- ½ cup chopped avocado
- 1 teaspoon fresh grated ginger
- 1 teaspoon lemon juice
- Ice cubes, optional
- ¼ cup whipped cream

Instructions:

1. Combine all of the ingredients in a blender.
2. Pulse several times, then blend for 30 to 60 seconds.
3. Add ice to thicken, if desired, and blend until smooth.
4. Pour into two glasses and top with whipped cream to serve.

Nutrition: 280 calories, 28g fat, 3g protein, 4g net carbs

Dessert and Drinks Recipes

Almond Butter Cookies

Servings: 8

Serving Size: 1 cookie

Prep Time: 10 minutes

Cook Time: 15 minutes

Ingredients:

- ½ cup almond butter
- 1 tablespoon coconut oil
- 2 large eggs
- 1 teaspoon vanilla extract
- 1 tablespoon coconut flour
- 1 teaspoon ground cinnamon
- 1 cup shredded unsweetened coconut
- ¼ cup chopped pecans

Instructions:

1. Preheat the oven to 350°F and line a baking sheet with parchment paper.
2. Stir together the almond butter, coconut oil, eggs, and vanilla extract.
3. Stir in the coconut flour and cinnamon until well combined.
4. Fold in the coconut and pecans then drop in rounded spoonfuls onto the baking sheet.
5. Flatten the balls slightly then bake for 12 to 14 minutes.

Nutrition: 115 calories, 10g fat, 3g protein, 2g net carbs

Dessert and Drinks Recipes

Blueberry Protein Smoothie

Servings: 2

Serving Size: ½ recipe

Prep Time: 5 minutes

Cook Time: 0 minutes

Ingredients:

- 1 ½ cups unsweetened almond milk
- ¼ cup canned coconut milk
- 1 scoop whey protein powder
- ¼ cup frozen blueberries
- 1 teaspoon powdered erythritol
- 1 teaspoon coconut oil
- Ice cubes, optional
- ¼ cup whipped cream

Instructions:

1. Combine all of the ingredients in a blender.
2. Pulse several times, then blend for 30 to 60 seconds.
3. Add ice to thicken, if desired, and blend until smooth.
4. Pour into two glasses and top with whipped cream to serve.

Nutrition: 235 calories, 18g fat, 13g protein, 6g net carbs

Dessert and Drinks Recipes

Coconut Brownies

Servings: 12

Serving Size: 1 brownie

Prep Time: 10 minutes

Cook Time: 30 minutes

Ingredients:

- ¾ cup unsweetened cocoa powder
- 2 large eggs
- 1 cup coconut oil, melted
- ½ cup canned coconut milk
- 2 teaspoons powdered stevia extract
- 1 cup almond flour
- ½ cup shredded unsweetened coconut
- ½ teaspoon baking soda

Instructions:

1. Preheat the oven to 350°F and grease a square baking dish.
2. Whisk together the cocoa powder, eggs, coconut oil, coconut milk, and stevia.
3. In a separate bowl, whisk together the almond flour, coconut, and baking soda.
4. Combine the two mixtures until smooth, then pour into the baking dish.
5. Bake for 30 minutes until the center is set, then cool completely before cutting.

Nutrition: 245 calories, 25.5g fat, 3.5g protein, 2g net carbs

Dessert and Drinks Recipes

Cherry Coconut Smoothie

Servings: 2

Serving Size: ½ recipe

Prep Time: 5 minutes

Cook Time: 0 minutes

Ingredients:

- 1 cup unsweetened almond milk
- ¼ cup canned coconut milk
- ¼ cup frozen cherries, unsweetened
- 2 tablespoons shredded coconut
- ¼ teaspoon vanilla extract
- Ice cubes, optional
- ¼ cup whipped cream

Instructions:

1. Combine all of the ingredients in a blender.
2. Pulse several times, then blend for 30 to 60 seconds.
3. Add ice to thicken, if desired, and blend until smooth.
4. Pour into two glasses and top with whipped cream to serve.

Nutrition: 160 calories, 15g fat, 2g protein, 4g net carbs

Dessert and Drinks Recipes

Strawberry Cheesecake Bombs

Servings: 10

Serving Size: 1 bomb

Prep Time: 10 minutes

Cook Time: 0 minutes

Ingredients:

- ¾ cup cream cheese, softened
- ¼ cup coconut oil, softened
- ½ cup fresh sliced strawberries
- 2 tablespoons powdered erythritol
- 2 teaspoons vanilla extract

Instructions:

1. Combine the cream cheese and coconut oil in a bowl and stir until smooth.
2. Mash the strawberries in a separate bowl then stir in the erythritol and vanilla extract.
3. Stir the mixture into the cream cheese mixture until well combined.
4. Beat with a hand mixer until fluffy, then spoon into silicone molds.
5. Freeze for about 2 hours or until firm. Enjoy cold.

Nutrition: 115 calories, 11.5g fat, 1.5g protein, 1g net carbs

Dessert and Drinks Recipes

Chocolate Green Smoothie

Servings: 2

Serving Size: ½ recipe

Prep Time: 5 minutes

Cook Time: 0 minutes

Ingredients:

- 1 ½ cups unsweetened almond milk
- 1 ½ cups fresh baby spinach
- ¼ cup frozen blueberries
- ½ cup canned coconut milk
- 1 scoop chocolate whey protein powder
- 1 tablespoon unsweetened cocoa powder
- 1 teaspoon powdered erythritol
- Ice cubes, optional
- ¼ cup whipped cream

Instructions:

1. Combine all of the ingredients in a blender.
2. Pulse several times, then blend for 30 to 60 seconds.
3. Add ice to thicken, if desired, and blend until smooth.
4. Pour into two glasses and top with whipped cream to serve.

Nutrition: 260 calories, 22.5g fat, 9g protein, 7g net carbs

Dessert and Drinks Recipes

Ginger Cookies

Servings: 16

Serving Size: 1 cookie

Prep Time: 10 minutes

Cook Time: 15 minutes

Ingredients:

- 1 cup coconut butter
- 1 large egg
- 1 teaspoon vanilla extract
- ½ cup powdered erythritol
- ½ teaspoon baking soda
- ½ tablespoon ground ginger
- 1 teaspoon ground turmeric
- Pinch salt

Instructions:

1. Preheat the oven to 350°F and line a baking sheet with parchment paper.
2. Combine the coconut butter, egg and vanilla extract in a food processor.
3. Blend until smooth, then blend in the erythritol, baking soda, and spices.
4. Shape the dough into 1-inch balls and place on the baking sheet.
5. Press flat slightly then bake for 10 to 15 minutes until browned.

Nutrition: 190 calories, 18g fat, 2.5g protein, 2g net carbs

Dessert and Drinks Recipes

<u>Kale Ginger Smoothie</u>

Servings: 2

Serving Size: ½ recipe

Prep Time: 5 minutes

Cook Time: 0 minutes

Ingredients:

- 2 cups fresh chopped kale
- ½ cup chopped cilantro
- 1 inch fresh ginger, grated
- 1 cup unsweetened almond milk
- 1 tablespoon coconut oil
- Ice cubes, optional
- ¼ cup whipped cream

Instructions:

1. Combine all of the ingredients in a blender.
2. Pulse several times, then blend for 30 to 60 seconds.
3. Add ice to thicken, if desired, and blend until smooth.
4. Pour into two glasses and top with whipped cream to serve.

Nutrition: 165 calories, 13g fat, 3g protein, 8.5g net carbs

Dessert and Drinks Recipes

Chocolate Peanut Butter Fat Bombs

Servings: 10

Serving Size: 1 fat bomb

Prep Time: 10 minutes

Cook Time: 0 minutes

Ingredients:

- ⅓ cup hemp seeds
- ¼ cup unsweetened cocoa powder
- ¼ cup powdered peanut butter
- ½ cup coconut oil
- 2 tablespoons heavy cream
- 1 teaspoon liquid stevia extract
- 1 teaspoon vanilla extract
- ⅓ cup shredded unsweetened coconut

Instructions:

1. Combine the cocoa powder, hemp seeds, and peanut butter powder in a food processor.
2. Add the coconut oil and pulse until it comes together in a thick paste.
3. Add the heavy cream, stevia, and vanilla, and blend until smooth.
4. Roll the mixture into 10 balls by hand.
5. Coat each ball in shredded coconut, then chill until firm.

Nutrition: 190 calories, 18g fat, 5.5g protein, 2g net carbs

Dessert and Drinks Recipes

Power Greens Smoothie

Servings: 2

Serving Size: ½ recipe

Prep Time: 5 minutes

Cook Time: 0 minutes

Ingredients:

- 1 ½ cups fresh spinach
- ½ cup fresh chopped kale
- 1 cup unsweetened almond milk
- ¼ cup canned coconut milk
- 1 scoop whey protein powder
- Ice cubes, optional
- ¼ cup whipped cream

Instructions:

1. Combine all of the ingredients in a blender.
2. Pulse several times, then blend for 30 to 60 seconds.
3. Add ice to thicken, if desired, and blend until smooth.
4. Pour into two glasses and top with whipped cream to serve.

Nutrition: 205 calories, 14.5g fat, 14g protein, 5.5g net carbs

Dessert and Drinks Recipes

<u>Cucumber Avocado Smoothie</u>

Servings: 2

Serving Size: ½ recipe

Prep Time: 5 minutes

Cook Time: 0 minutes

Ingredients:

- 1 cup coconut water
- ½ cup chopped avocado
- ½ cup diced cucumber (seedless)
- 2 tablespoons fresh chopped cilantro
- 1 tablespoon fresh lemon juice
- 2 teaspoons powdered erythritol
- Ice cubes, optional
- ¼ cup whipped cream

Instructions:

1. Combine all of the ingredients in a blender.
2. Pulse several times, then blend for 30 to 60 seconds.
3. Add ice to thicken, if desired, and blend until smooth.
4. Pour into two glasses and top with whipped cream to serve.

Nutrition: 150 calories, 12g fat, 2g protein, 5g net carbs

Conclusion

Congratulations! We have gone through this together and you made it to this juncture!

I can't tell you how excited I am for you to take the next step in your journey toward health and happiness. With the knowledge you've gained in reading this book plus the tools I've provided, you have everything you need to take back control of your life and of your health. Whether you're looking to lose weight or just boost your health and longevity, you're now fully equipped to make your dreams a reality!

Before I buzz off to write up my next piece of work for everyone, I want to give you a quick preview into the next few weeks of your life. As you get started with the first meal plan, you should expect a few hiccups. It will take time for you to recognize foods that are and are not keto-friendly, plus you may have to make some adjustments to your cooking style. I have complete confidence that you will learn quickly and come to find that following the ketogenic diet is not only easy, but delicious and satisfying as well!

Going keto might mean different things for you than it did for me, but I want to briefly highlight some of the amazing benefits you have to look forward to:

- Effective weight loss
- Increased fat burn
- Reduced risk for diabetes
- Better mood and concentration
- Improved energy levels
- Stabilized blood sugar levels

- Reduced blood pressure
- Protection against cancer
- Slowed neurological decline
- Longer lifespan
- Reduced inflammation
- Better, more restful sleep

Don't all of those benefits sound amazing? The best part is that you can enjoy all of them, just by sticking to the diet!

Keep in mind that every person's body responds differently to changes in diet and lifestyle. While you can expect to experience most of the benefits from this list eventually, it may not happen overnight. I will say it again, you may find that in switching to the ketogenic diet, your body goes through the transition phase which we all know now as "keto flu." Don't worry – these symptoms are temporary. If you stick to going keto, you'll feel better in no time!

Well, I hope that you feel ready and excited to give the ketogenic diet a try – I'm excited for you! Just to make sure that everything goes off without a hitch, I'm going to conclude with a quick Q&A. Here are some of the most frequently asked questions about the ketogenic diet:

Q: Is the ketogenic diet viable in the long term?

A: Before answering this question, you must remember that the ketogenic diet is not recommended for everyone. Talk to your doctor to make sure it is a safe choice for you. If it is, you can then start thinking about whether it is a good long-term choice based on convenience and results. For some people the ketogenic diet is a tool for weight loss, but they choose to return to a more moderate carb diet after they've achieved their goals simply because it is more convenient for them. There is no hard and fast evidence to suggest that the ketogenic diet is not a viable long-term diet, but it's different for everyone. For me, I have been on the keto diet for years, and am happy to say that it has definitely brought me more good than harm.

Q: What kind of exercise can I do on the ketogenic diet?

A: Adding exercise to your ketogenic diet can help to speed your weight loss and, depending what type of exercise you do, might help to preserve lean muscle mass as well. If you prefer cardiovascular exercises like running or biking, you shouldn't have too much trouble while following the ketogenic diet. If you're working out for more than an hour or going at a high pace, however, you might want to time your daily carb intake to coincide with your work out so you have the energy. Refer back to the section about the different types of ketogenic diet to learn more.

Q: Does the keto diet increase my risk for kidney stones?

A: The high protein nature of certain diets puts some people at risk for kidney stones. What you need to realize about the ketogenic diet, however, is that it is not a high-protein diet like many people assume it to be. It is a high-fat, moderate-protein, low-carb diet. As long as you stick to your macronutrient ratios, you should be fine.

Q: What happens if my weight loss plateaus – what do I do?

A: No matter what diet you choose to follow, it is natural for your weight to go through some ups and downs. If you find that your weight loss has stalled while you're following the ketogenic diet, there are a few things you can check. First, make sure your macronutrient ratios are correct. You may find that you're eating too many carbs or not enough protein. You should also make sure you're keeping your fluid balance and your electrolytes up. If you feel like you've strayed too far from the diet, simply start over with the first meal plan to get back on track. If you are deep in ketosis and you can really say that you have not strayed off the track one single bit, try adding some additional carbs for a couple of days. It might just be the catalyst to restart the weight loss whilst on the keto diet.

Q: If I am already thin but want to improve my health, will the keto diet work for me?

A: While many people switch to the ketogenic diet to lose weight, it can also be a tool for improving your health. If you are already at a healthy bodyweight, simply calculate your current energy requirements and adjust your macronutrient ratio accordingly for maintenance rather than weight loss.

Q: Do I have to track my calories and macros?

A: There is no hard and fast rule for how to follow the ketogenic diet – you are free to customize it according to your needs. While you might be able to get by without counting calories or tracking macros, you may find that your results are a little less consistent. The key to long-term success with the ketogenic diet is getting your body into a state of ketosis in the first place – this is where tracking calories and macros really comes in handy. Once your body is keto-adapted, however, you might be able to follow a more general approach and still see good results.

Q: Is high cholesterol on the ketogenic diet a problem?

A: This has always been the million dollar question, which is why it is left for the last. Just kidding! For about two-thirds of the people who go on the ketogenic diet, they encounter lowered overall cholesterol levels, better HDL and reduced LDL. For the remaining one-third, however, we see higher overall cholesterol levels, mainly due to a boost in the HDL segment, while LDL remains constant or slightly elevated.

The keyword here is "we," I too belong to this one-third. And I can tell you that it totally freaked me out in the beginning. I started reading up here and there, trying to find justification and explanation for this increase. I started to question the keto diet as well. I am glad I did the research, because it led me to the observation that while my overall levels were elevated, my other risk markers were dropping like flies. During the next two years into the diet, I still had what the medical world terms as elevated cholesterol levels, but my triglyceride levels were super optimal, while risk markers for inflammation and heart disease were also in the optimal range. It wasn't until about two years ago, when I was going for my annual medical checks that my lipid profile showed my cholesterol levels as being medically healthy.

Nothing changed for me during the years since I started the keto diet, I was still eating the same amount of fats and other macros, and putting in the workouts that I like. I wanted to share this bit with everyone because it can be terrifying to see your cholesterol levels go up when you are on a diet that is supposedly heart healthy. The trick here is to focus on your HDL numbers, as well as the particle size of your LDL. Larger LDL sizing is much better than small, dense oxidized LDL pellets.

Total cholesterol numbers do not mean much if it was brought on by an increase in your HDL numbers. Even when LDL increases, if tests show that the particle sizing is of the large, fluffy variety, you should not be alarmed. Cholesterol levels may take time to normalize, as they did for me. Just keep the faith and maintain course on the keto journey.

My personal thought, after much delving into related cholesterol research, was that the body was actually healing itself after my decades of carb-related damage. That, in my mind, was the probable reason why my cholesterol levels were elevated and remained that way for some time. It then normalized once it determined that the damage was repaired. For me, I always hope that anybody new on the keto diet would fall into the two-thirds majority. However, for anyone who is in the high cholesterol one-third minority, take heart in what I have shared, and be prepared to reap the benefits of the ketogenic diet!

An Important Added Note

As detailed above in the meal plan and recipe section, (I'm repeating here in case you missed it), as a bonus and to add more value to you, I have actually created what I find to be fairly useful recipe cards. These are great to print out for easy reference and come with full color pictures too! I have made recipe cards for about two dozen of the book's recipes and would like you to have them free! Just go on ahead below and go to the link. Follow the simple one step instruction and you will have the recipe cards emailed to you!

www.fcmediapublishing.com/recipecardsrw1

Easy-peasy to get to the link above! That is recipecards with a rw and finally a digit 1.

There will be other books coming out on the ketogenic diet from me, so do look out for them. In the meantime, if you have enjoyed this book, please do leave a review for me on Amazon and I would be most grateful!

Thank you, stay healthy and happy!

About The Author

Robert wasn't born with genetics predisposed toward weight gain, nor did he have big bones. He just happened to really like to eat, and eat what he liked. That would have not been a problem if the food available happened to be all healthy and nutritious. But healthy and nutritious seemed like the unicorn, elusive and rare, and most of it didn't seem that tasty then anyways.

It wasn't until his weight ballooned and he was beset by multiple health issues stemming from his poor diet and sedentary lifestyle that change was sort of forced upon him. Before this health alarm, he knew that something wasn't quite right when he puffed and wheezed after just a single flight of stairs, but as everyone is wont to do, the "nothing is going to happen to me" syndrome kicked in, and life just rolled on.

When he got hospitalized for dangerously high blood pressure, that was when something just changed, and he knew he had to get his act together. He researched like a mad man, given that his life was quite simply hanging on a couple of flimsy threads. He paid his dues and tried his hand at various different diets until finally, he chanced upon the ketogenic diet, and that was when he never looked back.

The health problems faded away, he got his body trim and fit, and more importantly, he felt great both on the inside and outside. A crusader and prophet of the ketogenic diet he is not, but he is ever willing to share how the diet can be beneficial and be a catalyst to a change for the better!

Resources

[1] "Overweight and Obesity Statistics." NIH.
<https://www.niddk.nih.gov/health-information/health-statistics/overweight-obesity>

[2] "Why Are Americans Obese?" Obesity in America.
<http://www.publichealth.org/public-awareness/obesity/>

[3] "What Happens to Unburned Carbohydrates?" Livestrong.
<http://healthyeating.sfgate.com/happens-unburned-carbohydrates-2461.html>

[4] Paoli, Antonio. "Ketogenic Diet for Obesity: Friend or Foe?"
International Journal of Environmental Research and Public Health. 2014
Feb; 11(2): 2092-2107.
<https://www.ncbi.nlm.nih.gov/pmc/articles/PMC3945587/>

[5] Sumithran P. "Ketosis and Appetite-Mediating Nutrients and Hormones
After Weight Loss." European Journal of Clinical Nutrition. 2013 Jul; 67(7):
759-64. <https://www.ncbi.nlm.nih.gov/pubmed/23632752>

[6] Veech RL. "The Therapeutic Implications of Ketone Bodies." PLEFA.
2004 Mar; 70(3): 309-19.
<https://www.ncbi.nlm.nih.gov/pubmed/14769489>

[7] Boden G. "Effect of a Low-Carb Diet on Appetite, Blood Glucose
Levels, and Insulin Resistance in Obese Patients with Type 2 Diabetes."
Annals of Internal Medicine. 2005 Mar; 142(6): 403-11.
<https://www.ncbi.nlm.nih.gov/pubmed/15767618>

[8] Hession M. "Systematic Review of Randomized Controlled Trials of
Low-Carbohydrate vs Low-Fat/Low-Calorie Diets in the Management of
Obesity and Its Comorbidities." Obes Rev. 2009 Jan; 10(1): 36-50.
<https://www.ncbi.nlm.nih.gov/pubmed/18700873>

[9] Zhou, Weihua. "The Calorically Restricted Ketogenic Diet, An Effective Alternative Therapy for Malignant Brain Cancer." Nutr Metab. 2007 Feb; 4: 5. <https://www.ncbi.nlm.nih.gov/pmc/articles/PMC1819381/>

[10] Choragiewicz, T. "Anticonvulsant and Neuroprotective Effects of the Ketogenic Diet." Przeql Lek. 2010; 67(30: 205-12. < https://www.ncbi.nlm.nih.gov/pubmed/20687386>

[11] "Diabetic Ketoacidosis." Mayo Clinic. <https://www.mayoclinic.org/diseases-conditions/diabetic-ketoacidosis/symptoms-causes/syc-20371551>

[12] Roussel, Mike. "Ask the Macro Manager: What is the Thermic Effects of Food?" Bodybuilding.com. <https://www.bodybuilding.com/fun/ask-the-macro-manager-what-is-thermic-effect.html>

[13] "Diabetes Complications." Healthline. <https://www.healthline.com/health/diabetes-complications>

[14] "Metabolic Syndrome." Mayo Clinic. <https://www.mayoclinic.org/diseases-conditions/metabolic-syndrome/symptoms-causes/syc-20351916>

[15] "Side Effects of a Ketogenic Diet." Diabetes.co.uk. <https://www.diabetes.co.uk/keto/side-effects-of-ketogenic-diet.html>

[16] "Determining Daily Calorie Needs." Free Dieting. <https://www.freedieting.com/calorie_needs.html>

Appendix A
Conversion Charts

Weight Conversions		
Metric	**Cups**	**Ounces**
15g	1 tablespoon	½ ounce
30g	⅛ cup	1 ounce
60g	¼ cup	2 ounces
115g	½ cup	4 ounces
170g	¾ cup	6 ounces
225g	1 cup	8 ounces
450g	2 cups	16 ounces

Volume Conversions		
Metric	**Cups**	**Ounces**
15 ml	1 tablespoon	½ fluid ounce
30 ml	2 tablespoons	1 fluid ounce
60 ml	¼ cup	2 fluid ounces
125 ml	½ cup	4 fluid ounces
180 ml	¾ cup	6 fluid ounces
250 ml	1 cup	8 fluid ounces
500 ml	2 cups	16 fluid ounces
1,000 ml	4 cups	1 quart

Oven Temperatures	
Celsius	**Fahrenheit**
95°C	200°F
130°C	250°F
150°C	300°F
160°C	325°F
175°C	350°F
190°C	375°F
200°C	400°F
230°C	450°F

Appendix B
Weekly Shopping List

Week 1 Shopping List

Meat and Eggs:

- Bacon, thick-cut – 23 slices
- Beef, ground (80% lean) – 8 ounces
- Chicken breasts, boneless – 12 ounces
- Chicken thighs, boneless – 1 ½ pounds
- Eggs – 33 large
- Lamb, ground – 1 pound
- Pork, tenderloin – 2 (6-ounce) chops
- Salmon – 2 (6-ounce) fillets
- Sausage, Italian – ½ pound
- Sausage, pork – 12 ounces
- Steak, sirloin – 4 ounces
- White fish – 1 pound

Dairy Products:

- Almond milk, unsweetened – ½ cup
- Butter – 12 tablespoons
- Cheddar cheese, shredded – 2 ½ cups
- Cream cheese – 1 ½ cups
- Heavy cream – 2 ⅓ cups
- Mayonnaise – ¼ cup
- Mexican cheese, shredded – 1 ounce

Dairy Products:

- Pepper jack cheese, cubed – 4 ounces
- Sour cream – 1 ⅓ cups
- Whipped cream – ¼ cup

Produce:

- Apple – 1 medium
- Avocado – 1 small, 3 medium
- Bell pepper, red – 1 medium
- Broccoli – 1 pound chopped
- Cauliflower – 2 medium heads
- Cilantro – 1 bunch
- Cucumber – ¼ cup
- Garlic – 1 head
- Ginger – 1 piece
- Green beans – 2 cups
- Jalapeno – 1
- Kale – 1 bunch
- Lemon – 1
- Lime – 2
- Mushrooms – 8 ounces
- Onion, green – 3 stalks
- Onion, yellow – 3 small, 3 medium
- Parsley – 1 bunch
- Romaine lettuce – 1 heart plus 1 cup
- Rosemary – 1 bunch
- Scallions – 1 stalk
- Spinach – 4 ½ cups

Produce:

- Tomato – 3 small, 3 medium
- Zucchini – 2 small

Pantry Staples:

- Almonds, whole – 1 cup plus 2 tablespoons
- Almond butter – 2 tablespoons
- Almond flour – ¼ cup
- Baking powder
- Baking soda
- Banana extract
- Broth, chicken – 3 ¼ cups
- Cayenne
- Chia seeds – 10 tablespoons
- Cocoa butter – ¼ cup
- Coconut cream – 1 ¼ cups
- Coconut flour – ½ cup
- Coconut milk, canned – 4 (14-ounce) cans
- Coconut oil
- Curry powder
- Dried thyme
- Ground cinnamon
- Ground cumin
- Ground flaxseed – 2 tablespoons
- Ground turmeric
- Liquid stevia extract
- Powdered stevia extract

Pantry Staples:

- Olive oil
- Paprika
- Pepper
- Powdered erythritol
- Psyllium husk powder
- Salt
- Vanilla extract
- Walnuts, toasted – 1 ounce
- White vinegar
- White wine, dry – ¼ cup

Week 2 Shopping List

Meat and Eggs:

- Bacon, thick-cut – 13 slices
- Beef, ground (80% lean) – 4 ounces
- Beef, ribeye – 2 (5-ounce) steaks
- Chicken thighs – 2 bone-in
- Eggs – 29 large
- Ham, deli – 4 ounces
- Lamb, bone-in chops – 12 ounces
- Pepperoni, diced – 2 ounces
- Pork, ground – 17 ounces
- Sausage, ground Italian – 8 ounces
- Turkey, smoked – 4 ounces
- White fish – 1 ½ pounds fillets

Dairy Products:

- Almond milk, unsweetened – 5 cups
- Avocado oil mayonnaise – ¼ cup
- Butter – 9 tablespoons
- Cheddar cheese, shredded – 1 cup
- Cream cheese – 1 cup
- Goat cheese – 3 ounces
- Greek yogurt, full-fat – ¾ cup
- Heavy cream – 2 ¾ cups
- Mayonnaise –
- Mozzarella, shredded – 2 ¼ cups
- Sour cream – 2 tablespoons
- Whipped cream – 1 cup

Robert Wilson

Produce:

- Avocado – 4 small, 2 medium
- Bell pepper, red – 1 small, 1 medium
- Blueberries, frozen – ¼ cup
- Broccoli – 1 pound chopped
- Cauliflower – 1 small head, 1 medium head
- Celery – 1 small stalk
- Coleslaw mix – 2 cups
- Garlic – 1 head
- Ginger – 1 piece
- Green beans – 2 cups
- Jalapeno – 3
- Lemon – 4
- Mushrooms – 8 ounces plus ½ cup
- Onions, green – 4 stalks
- Onion, yellow – 3 small, 1 medium
- Parsley – 4 tablespoons
- Raspberries – 5 whole
- Romaine – 4 ½ cups
- Salsa – 1 container
- Scallions – 1 bunch
- Snap peas – 1 cup
- Spinach – 3 cups
- Spring greens – 6 cups
- Strawberries, frozen – 5 whole
- Tomatoes – 1 medium
- Zucchini – 1 medium

Pantry Staples:

- Almond butter – 2 tablespoons
- Almond flour – 3 ½ cups
- Baking powder
- Baking soda
- Balsamic vinegar
- Broth, chicken – 2 ¾ cups
- Capers – 2 tablespoons
- Chia seeds – ¾ cup
- Chili powder
- Coconut, shredded unsweetened – ¾ cup
- Coconut flour – ¾ cup
- Coconut milk, canned – 4 (14-ounce) cans
- Coconut oil
- Coffee
- Dijon mustard
- Dried Italian seasoning
- Dried oregano
- Garlic powder
- Ground cumin
- Ground flaxseed – 2 tablespoons
- Liquid stevia extract
- Olive oil
- Onion powder
- Orange extract
- Pepper
- Poppy seeds – 3 tablespoons
- Powdered erythritol
- Psyllium husk powder

Pantry Staples:

- Salt
- Sesame seeds – ½ cup
- Soy sauce
- Unsweetened cocoa powder – ¾ cup
- Vanilla extract
- Walnuts, toasted – 1 tablespoon
- Whey protein powder, chocolate – 2 scoops
- Whey protein powder, vanilla – 3 scoop

Week 3 Shopping List

Meat and Eggs:

- Bacon, thick-cut – 4 ounces plus 11 slices
- Beef, chuck roast – 1 pound
- Beef, ground (80% lean) – 25 ounces
- Eggs – 23 large
- Halibut – 4 (6-ounce) fillets
- Pepperoni, diced – 2 ounces
- Pork, loin chop – 1 (5-ounce) chop
- Roast beef, sliced – 4 ounces
- Sausage, breakfast – 12 ounces
- Sausage, chorizo – 12 ounces
- White fish, fillets – 12 ounces

Dairy Products:

- Almond milk, unsweetened – 4 ¼ cups
- Blue cheese – 2 ounces
- Butter – ¾ cup
- Cheddar cheese, shredded – ¾ cup
- Cream cheese – ½ cup
- Greek yogurt, full-fat – ¼ cup
- Heavy cream – 3 tablespoons
- Mozzarella, shredded – 1 ½ cups
- Parmesan cheese – ½ cup
- Pepper jack cheese, shredded – 2 ounces
- Sour cream – 9 tablespoons
- Queso fresco – 2 ounces
- Whipped cream – 1 cup

Produce:

- Asparagus – 10 ounces
- Avocado – 4 small, 2 medium
- Bell pepper, red – 3 small, 1 medium
- Blueberries – ½ cup
- Cabbage – 1 small head
- Cauliflower – 2 small heads
- Cherries, frozen – ¼ cup
- Cilantro – 1 bunch
- Cucumber, seedless – ½ cup
- Garlic – 1 head
- Ginger – 1 piece
- Kale – ½ cup
- Lemon – 2
- Mushrooms – 1 cup
- Onion, green – 2 stalks
- Onion, red – 1 large
- Onion, yellow – 3 small, 2 medium
- Oregano – 1 bunch
- Parsley – 1 bunch
- Romaine – 1 ½ cups
- Spaghetti squash – 3 cups
- Spinach – 1 ½ cups
- Thyme – 1 bunch
- Tomatoes – 4 cherry
- Zucchini – 2 medium

Pantry Staples:

- Almond butter – ½ cup
- Almond flour – ¾ cup
- Baking powder
- Baking soda
- Broth, beef – ½ cup
- Chia seeds – ¼ cup
- Chili powder
- Chilis, canned – 2 tablespoons
- Cocoa nibs – 50g
- Coconut, shredded unsweetened – 1 ½ cups
- Coconut butter – ½ cup
- Coconut flour – 1 tablespoons
- Coconut oil – 2 jars
- Coconut milk – 1 (14-ounce) can
- Coconut water
- Diced tomatoes – 1 (14-ounce) can
- Dried Italian seasoning
- Dried oregano
- Dried thyme
- Garlic powder
- Ground cinnamon
- Ground cumin
- Ground flaxseed – 2 tablespoons
- Liquid stevia extract
- Macadamia nuts – 1 ounce
- Olive oil
- Paprika
- Peanut butter – 2 tablespoons

Pantry Staples:

- Pecans, chopped – ¼ cup
- Pepper
- Powdered erythritol
- Psyllium husk powder
- Pumpkin seeds – ½ cup
- Rice vinegar
- Salt
- Soy sauce
- Sriracha
- Tomato sauce, low-carb – ⅔ cup
- Unsweetened cocoa powder – 2 tablespoons
- Vanilla extract
- Whey protein powder – 5 scoops
- Whey protein powder, chocolate – 2 scoops
- Xanthan gum

Appendix C
Easy Recipe Directory

Breakfast	Calories	Fat (g)	Protein (g)	Carbs (g)
Biscuits with Gravy	425	36	22	2
Mexican-Style Scrambled Eggs	470	39	26.5	6
Bacon-Wrapped Spinach Quiches	300	22.5	20	4
Breakfast Pizza Skillet	595	45	37	9
Bacon Zucchini Hash	415	32	22	9.5
Breakfast Pockets	440	33.5	32	2.5
Chocolate Coconut Pancakes	535	40	27	8.5
Cheddar Sausage Omelet	545	43	33	5
Chocolate Mocha Chia Pudding	320	25	15.5	6.5
Vanilla Protein Smoothie	500	43	24	4.5
Jalapeno Cheddar Waffles	265	13	23	9.5
Lamb and Cheddar Breakfast Casserole	425	28	37	4.5
Raspberry Walnut Smoothie Bowl	485	35	27	11
Chorizo Egg Skillet	450	37	23.5	11
Veggie Mozzarella Quiche	305	24	15	6.5
Chocolate Chip Waffles	505	31	40	11
Spiced Almond Muffins	295	24.5	12.5	6
Cheddar Sausage Egg Muffins	445	35.5	25.5	5
Peanut Butter Breakfast Smoothie	500	36.5	33	10.5
Omelet with Bacon and Peppers	425	29.5	30	6
Single-Serve French Toast	465	40	15.5	6.5

Lunch	Calories	Fat (g)	Protein (g)	Carbs (g)
Fried White Fish Cakes	430	30	33	3.5
Creamy Fish Chowder	360	26.5	21	6
Creamy Cauliflower Soup	285	20	13	10.5
Warm Zucchini Walnut Salad	450	45	9.5	4.5
Spinach Goat Cheese Pie	445	35.5	21.5	6
Easy Egg Salad	300	24	18	3
Apple Walnut Salad	445	40.5	11	12
Spinach and Steak Salad	460	31	37.5	5
BLT Sandwich	440	35.5	19	10.5
Pork Egg Roll Bowl	460	34.5	28	6
Beefy Cheddar Tacos	660	52	35	10
Hearty Hamburger Salad	480	37	29	3.5
Beefy Cabbage Stew	635	44	43.5	10
Pepperoni Pan Pizza	450	35	25	3.5
Gyro Salad with Avocado Tzatziki	485	29	45	5.5
Beef and Cheese Taco Skillet	475	33	29	12
Ham and Turkey Club Salad	355	26	24.5	6
Quick Roast Beef Casserole	405	26.5	38.5	5
Beef and Veggie Soup	395	21.5	41.5	6.5
Meaty Pizza Casserole	500	35	35	8.5
Cheddar-Stuffed Burgers	500	40	32.5	2

Dinner	Calories	Fat (g)	Protein (g)	Carbs (g)
Shrimp Zoodle Alfredo	335	18.5	31	11
Seared Salmon with Sautéed Kale	475	29.5	40	14
Dijon-Baked Salmon	365	18	48	2.5
Broccoli White Fish Casserole	640	45	48	8.5
Parmesan Crusted Halibut	565	46	34	1.5
Shrimp Scampi with Spaghetti Squash	325	16.5	32.5	8
Rosemary Apple Pork Tenderloin	565	33	54	9.5
Enchilada Chicken Bake	580	43.5	39	4.5

Coconut Chicken Curry	500	36	35.5	7
Pork-Stuffed Zucchini Boats	570	41.5	39	8.5
Sausage and Cabbage Skillet	315	21	20	9.5
Pesto Grilled Pork Chops	590	50	32	1
Pan-Seared Lemon Rosemary Chicken	465	24.5	52	4
Beef and Mushroom Stroganoff	625	51	31	11
Grilled Steak Kebabs	365	21	34	9
Lamb Chops with Herb Butter	560	40	39	8
Cauliflower Fried Rice with Beef	550	43	26	12
Bacon-Wrapped Stuffed Meatballs	575	41	43	8.5
Ribeye Steak with Green Beans	475	36	27	5
Cauliflower and Steak Skillet	405	25	36.5	5.5
Broccoli Cheddar Casserole with Lamb	610	40.5	52	5.5
Snacks	**Calories**	**Fat (g)**	**Protein (g)**	**Carbs (g)**
Guacamole Deviled Eggs	185	15	12	2
Curry Spiced Almonds	155	14	5	2
Chia Peanut Butter Bites	110	8	2	7
Cheesy Sausage Dip	170	15	7	2
Salted Kale Chips	75	7	1	3
Bacon Jalapeno Quick Bread	225	19	8	3
Toasted Pumpkin Seeds	100	8.5	5.5	0.5
Bacon-Wrapped Burger Bites	150	10	16	0.5
Almond Sesame Crackers	145	12.5	5	2
Cauliflower Cheese Dip	75	6	2.5	2
Deviled Eggs with Bacon	145	11	8.5	3
Coleslaw with Avocado Dressing	100	6	3	6
Creamsicle Fat Bombs	155	17	1	0.5
Baked Cauliflower Bites	100	4.5	6	4
Bacon-Wrapped Shrimp	100	6	9	0.5
Macadamia Blueberry Squares	175	18	1	2
Pepperoni Pizza Dip	290	26	8.5	6.5

Robert Wilson

Chia Coconut Bites	160	16.5	1.5	0.5
Lemon Blueberry Snack Bread	165	11	10	4.5
Cocoa Chocolate Fat Bombs	100	11	0.5	0.5
Pepperoni Pizza Chips	190	16	12	0.5

Desserts Drinks	Calories	Fat (g)	Protein (g)	Carbs (g)
Coconut Chia Pudding	225	20.5	4.5	3
Banana Lime Smoothie	250	24	3	3
Almond Cinnamon Bars	200	22	2	2
Vanilla Almond Butter Smoothie	240	16.5	16	4.5
Sweet Cinnamon Bread	155	12	4.5	4
Chocolate Protein Smoothie	150	8.5	12	6
Lemon Poppy Ice Cream	215	21	3	2.5
Strawberry Lemon Smoothie	145	11	2.5	8
Vanilla White Chocolate Fat Bombs	140	14	0	0
Creamy Avocado Smoothie	280	28	3	4
Almond Butter Cookies	115	10	3	2
Blueberry Protein Smoothie	235	18	13	6
Coconut Brownies	245	25.5	3.5	2
Cherry Coconut Smoothie	160	15	2	4
Strawberry Cheesecake Bombs	115	11.5	1.5	1
Chocolate Green Smoothie	260	22.5	9	7
Ginger Cookies	190	18	2.5	2
Kale Ginger Smoothie	165	13	3	8.5
Chocolate Peanut Butter Fat Bombs	190	18	5.5	2
Power Greens Smoothie	205	14.5	14	5.5
Cucumber Avocado Smoothie	150	12	2	0